PRAISE

Peter Dooley has given my wife and me the ability to recognize the patterns that obstruct our communication. This content has allowed us to correct our behavioral patterns during communication and increase our ability to communicate effectively. With Peter's help, we have realized the importance of clarifying messages instead of making assumptions. Along with improving our communication, we recognize the importance of passing down effective communication to our children. Peter is gifted at recognizing what hinders communication and offers solutions for improvement. Peter's insight into why we communicate the way we do is interesting and helpful to improve the communication process. There are a million self-help books that promise to change your life but Peter's method is simple, and we were able to apply the techniques immediately. With his help, we have learned techniques that will benefit our marriage forever. —*Tom and Danielle Kutter*

Every day we communicate in our relationships, whether good or bad. Most of the time, we do not pay attention. Peter lifts the veil off healthy communication and enriches our lives.

In class, Peter uses the material he has written to impress upon participants the correct way to communicate and to clarify what we are saying or hearing. It is a detailed look at how we communicate, as well as how our words affect others. — *Scott Wood*

This book is full of information that will force you to ask certain questions but answer them as well. The text flows and progresses well, moving from a foundational principle which details structured communication, to offering great tools like the debriefing guide. It also uses cases that the class can relate to. There are even small homework assignments that prompt self-reflection of covered material.

As a participant of this class/reader of the material, you'll quickly find you are not the only one who is going (or has gone) down the road you're currently traveling on. This communication guide is a road-map to successfully reaching your destination of blissful times through healthy communication.

If you aren't up for a healthy challenge, this is not for you. On the contrary, if you attend this class wholeheartedly, seeking to improve your communication, it will change your life. In my opinion, the principles this class teaches are simple but can be very challenging for those who are not willing to accept them. Studying this material has allowed me to achieve personal growth and success. I've applied these principles in both my personal and professional life. The principles are foolproof between individuals that are honest with one another.

Peter conveys the material to the class participants in a very smooth, concise, and patient way. Unless the class is addressing an area of focus that leads you to become defensive (your opportunity to improve communication), you'll yearn for more each and every time.

This book is a must-have tool and investment for any loving relationship regardless of age.

—*Craig Dooley*

Using his background in the healthcare industry and his life experience, Peter is able to bring out common pitfalls and solutions to daily communication. While my wife and I approached this material primarily to benefit our relationship, the concepts can easily be extended to all forms of

relationships including coworkers, parent/child, employee/manager, etc. Peter did a great job of pointing out subtle nuances that were acting as barriers to more effective communication and using that awareness to help us overcome those barriers.
—*James and Erin B.*

We have known Peter since early 2000; he's been a close family friend and Brother in Christ. Peter and his wife Christina have watched our family go through great times and hard times.

We were first introduced to their communication model in 2016 and started attending the meetings in the early part of 2017.

It was very difficult for us as a family at first, because we simply didn't know how dysfunctional our communication was. The classes not only helped us to understand that we weren't the only ones who were having these issues, but to hear how the tool helped impact other people's lives, and the ideas that were shared were very helpful.

We've since moved to Chiangmai, Thailand and still utilize this tool as much as possible.

We are still a work in progress, and we still rely very much on this tool as Peter and Christina have been so kind as to bless our family with an individual packet of our own.

I can't even begin to express how grateful we are for this tool. It has helped our family in so many ways. — *The Hall Family*

We had the privilege of being in Peter's class. We have been married for 35 years, and we have had our ups and downs.

We even came close to divorce several times. Peter approached us about meeting and going through a communication class because he noticed that so many people lacked the ability to get their message across to each other without so many misperceptions, which in turn causes so much confusion and pain. When Peter first gave us the Personal Evaluation Sheet, I thought to myself that most of my answers would be no and my husband's would be yes; to my surprise I had a lot of yes answers too, so I knew we had to go deeper. Peter has the ability to make you think and bring you straight to where the problems started. For some this is not easy to face; being in class with other couples, and realizing that you are not alone makes it easier to face. We help each other get an understanding with Peter's help, because sometimes we get stuck on finding the right way to communicate, and after he explains understanding becomes easier. One of the best tools is the Debriefing, which is usually done after discussion of whatever situation arises. You get to see yourself through someone else's eyes. This is a life-changing class. Now we think before we throw out words that are hurtful to each other because once you say those painful words, you can't take them back. Peter teaches us how to communicate with our family and people in general. Watching how far we have all come from the beginning until now, gives us all new hope because now we understand where the pain and hurt come from, and now we can help each other and other people as well. I would definitely do this class again. Peter is saving relationships! —*John and Claudette*

I Hear You

Copyright ©2018 Peter E. Dooley

All rights reserved.

This book or any portion thereof may not be reproduced or used in any manner whatsoever without the express written permission of the author except for the use of brief quotations in a book review.

Printed in the United States of America

First Printing, May 2018

ISBN-13: 978-1717338419

Book Publishing Services: WritersTablet.org

    Editor assigned: M. Malcolm

    Illustrator assigned: H. Workman

    Cover designer assigned: D. Vasiljevic

Cover Photograph: Wavebreakmedia

All Scripture quotations, unless otherwise indicated, are taken from the New International Version (NIV): Scripture taken from The Holy Bible, New International Version ®. Copyright© 1973, 1978, 1984, 2011 by Biblica, Inc.™. Used by permission of Zondervan.

This book is dedicated to Tina, my darling wife. You are still the love of my life. Thank you for being my go-to girl.

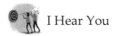 I Hear You

TABLE OF CONTENTS

PREFACE	1
ACKNOWLEDGEMENTS	6
INTRODUCTION	7
PERSONAL EVALUATION INSTRUCTIONS	15
PERSONAL EVALUATION OF YOUR COMMUNICATION	16
PERSONAL EVALUATION OF YOUR COMMUNICATION	18
COMMUNICATION GROUND RULES	20
DEFINITIONS	22
DEBRIEFING INSTRUCTIONS	25
DEBRIEFING RECORD	28
FEELING WORDS	30
EXAMPLES OF FEELING WORDS	31
CASE STUDY INSTRUCTIONS	33
COMMUNICATION GOALS	34
FOUNDATIONAL PRINCIPLE *(Core Concept)*	36
EXPRESSIONS OF FEELING	38
THE KEY TO EMOTIONAL HEALING *(Lighting the Path)*	40

 I Hear You

CHALLENGE	45
CASE STUDY *(The Dinner Invitation)*	46
HOW DO I LOVE ME? *(Protecting our Self-Esteem and Self-image)*	48
TEST 1	52
MODEL 1: EFFECTIVE COMMUNICATION	54
MODEL 2: INEFFECTIVE COMMUNICATION	56
TRUST THE PROCESS *(How Does It Flow?)*	63
THE NEGATIVE IMPACT OF ANXIETY ON COMMUNICATION	66
WHO AM I? *(Understanding Your Personality Type)*	72
THE ATTACKER	73
THE SPONGE	77
THE OSTRICH	78
THE ROAD RUNNER	80
THE DIPLOMAT	82
WHOSE MESSAGE IS IT? *(Who Has the Right to Define It?)*	85
WHO DID IT? *(Who Is Responsible?)*	89
TEST 2	92
THE BIG BANG *(The Most Negative Cycle of Hurt)*	94

 I Hear You

CASE STUDY *(The Toilet Paper Incident)*	95
GOD'S GIFT TO MAN *(The Ability to Soothe Hurt)*	102
CASE STUDY *(Selective Soothing)*	103
NOTHING MORE THAN FEELINGS *(Hearing Spoken Feelings)*	107
ATTACK VS. OPINION	111
SENSITIVE OR INSENSITIVE?	113
EMOTIONAL BURDEN VS. EMOTIONAL STARVATION *(Insensitivity)*	115
CASE STUDY *(Where is the Love?)*	116
THE STRUGGLING MIND *(The Product of Mistrust)*	127
CASE STUDY *(The Aftermath of Hurt)*	130
REMOVING THE CORK *(Revealing One's Hurt)*	135
COMPOUNDING THE HURT *(Spitefulness)*	139
THE DEVIL'S MESSAGE *(Brainwashing Ourselves)*	143
CASE STUDY *(Help Me See Clearly)*	146
HELP ME UNDERSTAND *(Clarify to Know)*	152
THE HARDENED HEART *(Solidifying Premature Conclusions)*	156

 I Hear You

CASE STUDY *(I Want It My Way)*	159
CUTTING THE CORD *(Forgiving)*	163
THE NEGATIVE TILT *(Failing to Take Responsibility)*	168
HONESTY *(Pure Honest Conduct)*	172
CASE STUDY *(Tell Me the Truth)*	175
IMPERFECT PERFECTION *(Trying to Be Perfect)*	177
CONTAINMENT BREACH *(Taming Hurtful Words)*	181
SHOCKING ELECTRONICS *(Texts and Emails)*	185
RIGHTFULLY WRONG *(The Need to be Right)*	190
CASE STUDY *(You First)*	192
FOUNDATIONAL PRINCIPLE *(Core Concept)*	199
REMEMBER THE MODEL	203
MODEL UTILIZATION	203
CONCLUDING WORDS *(It's in Your Hands)*	206
APPENDIX A	208
EXPRESSIONS OF FEELING	208
ATTACK VS. OPINION	209
APPENDIX B	210
TEST 1	210
TEST 2	212

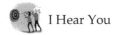 I Hear You

APPENDIX C	214
CASE STUDY *(The Dinner Invitation)*	214
CASE STUDY *(The Toilet Paper Incident)*	214
CASE STUDY *(Selective Soothing)*	215
CASE STUDY *(Where is the Love?)*	216
CASE STUDY *(The Aftermath of Hurt)*	218
CASE STUDY *(Help Me See Clearly)*	221
CASE STUDY *(I Want It My Way)*	221
CASE STUDY *(Tell Me the Truth)*	222
CASE STUDY *(You First)*	222
APPENDIX D	224
COURSE EVALUATION	224

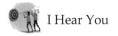 I Hear You

PREFACE

Relationships all around us are failing at a rapid rate. There is a hunger for tools that can aid us in the skill of relating to one another—tools that will allow us to thrive and grow together in love and understanding instead of simply tolerating each other until we cannot bear it anymore. Most of us have come out of households that offer very little formal training in the art of skillful, respectful communication. We usually leave our parents' home equipped with that which we have observed as well as fallen victim to during the most important developmental years of our lives. Without proper corrective training, we simply repeat the patterns to which we were exposed. The observed patterns—positive or negative—quickly become ingrained into our behaviors.

As we begin to relate to people outside our core family we quickly discover that people communicate differently. That difference can sometimes present challenges. The adaptive change necessary in order to respectfully communicate with others who embrace differing patterns of communication can sometimes prove to be a

daunting task. We may later discover that there were some unhealthy communication patterns learned during our time spent at home. Learning to listen and respond effectively can prove to be difficult since our established patterns of behavior most often feel proper. This is primarily because most of us have utilized our current pattern all of our lives. Reacting to stimuli simply requires emotion and words formulated without thought, but it takes intelligence and self-control to respond in an appropriate manner.

It behooves us to become vigilant in regards to the negative elements we inject into our relationships via the things we say and do. Some fail to look and therefore never discover the ineffective elements in their communication.

They simply stand idly by as their relationships are repeatedly consumed by the cancer of ineffective communication.

Matthew 13: 3-9 is often referred to as the parable of the sower. In this parable the bible states: "Then he told them many things in parables, saying: "A farmer went out to sow his seed. As he was scattering the seed, some fell along the path, and the birds came and ate it up. Some fell on rocky

 I Hear You

places, where it did not have much soil. It sprang up quickly, because the soil was shallow. But when the sun came up, the plants were scorched, and they withered because they had no root. Other seed fell among thorns, which grew up and choked the plants. Still other seed fell on good soil, where it produced a crop—a hundred, sixty or thirty times what was sown. Whoever has ears, let them hear." In this parable, in order for the sown seed to take root and mature to the point of yielding fruit, it needed nutrient-rich, absorbent soil. The content of this book is comparable to the seed sown in the parable. Simply reading the contents herein does not offer the guarantee that the change necessary to heal infected relationships will take place. We must be willing to look closely at our individual hearts—the soil—and determine if we are willing and ready to exert the necessary effort to establish understanding and produce change. Please read this material with the intention of gaining a better understanding of some of the complexities associated with relating to others and learning how to improve upon your responses when presented with some of these dynamics. Placing your focus on using the information to fix someone else may cause you to lose direction. If you are committed to

discovering the pitfalls of negative communication and to replacing those elements with growth-yielding tools, this book is for you. If not, the time spent reading the words of this book will likely be rendered unproductive.

The most precious commodity we have are our loved ones, especially our children. We must make an effort not to embrace misdirection while we simply react in an uncontrolled manner to words and actions that stir our emotions. Someone who views us as a role model is always perched on an observatory platform utilizing their visual and auditory senses to absorb the examples we display. Choose to represent yourself in a manner that illustrates contemplated, purposeful, effective choices when you engage with the people with whom you come in contact as you journey through life. It is your positive, loving example that will empower those around you and arm them in the fight against the cancer that consumes relationships—ineffective communication.

It is my hope that having read the words within this book you will come to realize that you are totally equipped to fight and win the war against the cancer that consumes relationships. My hope is

 I Hear You

that you will identify and begin to replace any element of unhealthy, ineffective communication that you discover with healthy, respectful alternatives. Open your heart. Allow your loved ones to see who you are. Commit to learning how to use the new tools and techniques found herein. Allow the force of change to move you in new directions. Change your paradigm.

ACKNOWLEDGEMENTS

All thanks to the Great God almighty, the creator of knowledge and wisdom, for directing my steps and guiding my thoughts.

The completion of this book was made easier by the involvement of some key individuals whose contributions are greatly appreciated and sincerely acknowledged.

To the Baxter, Dooley, Hall, Kutter, Washington, and Wood families: Thank you for being willing to embrace the principles laid forth in this book and applying them to your lives. Whether you were 100% successful with your attempts or not, thank you for your trying to implement those concepts you deemed beneficial. My love for you is real.

To my family members: Thank you for your love and support. The appreciation for the countless hours we have spent together examining and making application of the content in this book goes beyond what words can express.

 I Hear You

INTRODUCTION

Ineffective communication can be hurtful. However, it is important to realize that communication will never be perfect. Therefore, we should not expect it to be. When evaluating our communication, much emphasis should be placed on the following:

- Trying to gain an understanding of how our words and actions complicate the process.
- Gaining an understanding of the problems generated from our communication style.
- Knowing how to go about taking responsibility for our contribution or the lack thereof.

While acknowledging that there is a level of difficulty involved in limiting our response to some emotions, the goal is to limit any response that is emotionally charged.

The absence of communication or its delay is equal to or worse than ineffective communication. It allows issues to fester, which leads to other misperceptions. When we choose not to talk

because we are frustrated or otherwise, we contribute to the demise of the relationship.

It is unreasonable to expect that someone can know what you are feeling without you properly stating it.

One's display of anger does not state what one is feeling. Displays of anger are nothing less than threatening behaviors. If you desire to protect your relationships, I am suggesting that you begin asking questions. Direct them to the person who is the original source of the concern. Make absolutely sure you understand what you are responding to. This should be done before sending your feedback. Evaluate your emotional state before initiating or responding to communication when your feelings are stirred.

Emotions make a poor engine because they will usually run the train right off the track.

Other than conveying information, the primary goal of communication should be to avoid or repair hurt. When conveying information, messages should be formulated to deliver concise thoughts and should therefore be worded carefully to accomplish that goal. The inclusion of data not pertinent to the immediate topic can add confusion

 I Hear You

and has the potential to skew the message. Skewed messages can lead to indignation on the part of the receiver. Indignation can, in turn, lead to anger and frustration. Anger and frustration will tax the communication process.

Not all, but some hurt people tend to think unclearly and therefore require an additional measure of grace. This fact makes it important to give careful consideration to removing the hurt as quickly as possible. When hurt, people tend to focus on offensive actions before hearing spoken words. This makes it all the more imperative that we avoid verbally attacking someone when we feel hurt or frustration due to his or her actions. We must first thoroughly assess the intentions of others before allowing our actions to deliver a hurtful blow.

During the early part of this conversation it is important to convey to the receiver what happened and the feelings aroused by that action. A person experiencing hurt may not be able to address another person's feelings. One must quickly address the hurt and then convey the intended message afterwards.

 I Hear You

Addressing the pain caused by the offense will quickly deflate the inflated balloon of emotions and allow the offended party to focus on spoken words.

It is not typical for someone to respond to an apology or kind word with aggression or animosity. One's negative reaction to a present action or statement is usually tied to something that occurred earlier in life. It was probably improperly addressed, stored away as hurt, then occasionally revisited. Revisiting the emotions originating from hurt will compress them, causing them to become poised for an explosive release. Taking time to discover where the feelings originate enhances understanding and limits the intensity of the feelings. We must become skilled at bringing topics into focus so the receiver can have an opportunity to properly address them. Both parties must target the hasty removal of the hurt feelings before pursuing normal conversation. Failure to do this can lead to more intense feelings of indignation. If someone is unaware of your hurt, approaching that person in anger will be viewed as an attack and will block your intended message, especially when it is done in the presence of others. If you are in the pattern of aggressively pursuing

 I Hear You

your loved one in an effort to uncover a feeling you suspect is there after being alerted by a familiar verbal or nonverbal cue, I am suggesting that you stop that today. Simply share your observation, then ask if he or she is willing to share the feeling. That individual needs time to be introspective, identify what is being felt, and then carefully choose words to convey those feelings respectfully. This is a skill that will never be mastered by that individual if you continue to disrupt the process.

As you read through this book, you will notice that it is written in a modular format to facilitate its utilization by groups that meet periodically. These segments provide members of the group with reasonable stopping points. It can also be read straight through as you would any other book. If you read it straight through, you may notice repetition, which intentionally reinforces certain concepts.

The questionnaires found after the introduction are to be completed prior to reading any of the modules since the information you read will likely influence your answers to the questions. Try to make application of the concepts over time. After reading the book, you are encouraged to answer

 I Hear You

the questionnaires again and compare the new answers with the initial ones.

You will encounter tools designed to help you improve your communication as well as expose those areas where you can improve. Each tool has instructions regarding its proper utilization. You will also encounter definitions that ease the understanding of the terminology used in the book. You may want to keep a bible at hand, since you will encounter a fair amount of scripture taken from the New International Version.

Whether reading individually or as part of a group, you are encouraged to give thought to the influences that have molded your present communication style. Share the concepts with those with whom you have close relationships. Most readers will see themselves as well as others at some point in the material.

The bible teaches us to love, honor, respect, and forgive. It teaches us to be unselfish. These godly principles, when applied to our communication, bring harmony. The active question this book will answer is "How do we apply these principles to our communication?"

Communication that is ineffective causes misunderstandings. These misunderstandings sow seeds of disrespect that, when fully developed, give rise to deeply rooted feelings of hurt and humiliation. It is responsible for the death of what might otherwise be harmonious relationships. It is my intent that this book will be something we can routinely utilize to expose and combat this deadly foe.

All tools, questionnaires, and surveys can be found at www.PeterEDooley.com.

The underlying principle of this book is that improved communication results in improved personal relationships. At the same time, it is important to understand that your personal security has to be your priority. If you are in a situation where your life is in danger, such as a physically abusive relationship, do not delay separation in order to put these principles into practice. The first thing you should do is seek refuge in a local shelter or speak with a professional who can help you be safe.

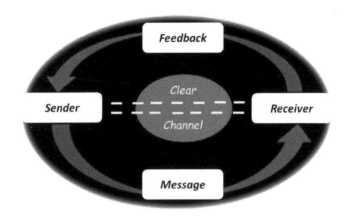

COMMUNICATION MODEL

1. **Sender** – The owner of the message being discussed.

2. **Message** – The information conveyed via verbal or nonverbal stimuli.

3. **A Clear Channel** – The unimpeded path through which the message travels.

4. **Receiver** – The recipient of the verbal or nonverbal message.

5. **Feedback** – The verbal or nonverbal reply pertaining to the content of the received message.

 I Hear You

PERSONAL EVALUATION INSTRUCTIONS

The Self-Evaluation pages are to be completed individually as soon as possible then kept for future reference. It is an honest evaluation of whether or not these patterns exist in your communication. Simply circle YES or NO. After completing them, it is recommended, if you are married, that you ask your spouse if they see you in the same manner that you see yourself. We often do not see our communication flaws and it is good for us to have honest, loving feedback. Do not become angry at your spouse for telling you the truth; simply become aware.

 I Hear You

PERSONAL EVALUATION OF YOUR COMMUNICATION

1. Do you shut down in silence? **(yes or no)**
2. Do you modify your behavior in the relationship when you are unsuccessful at communicating your view or you believe you have not been heard? **(yes or no)**
3. Do you rage? **(yes or no)**
4. Do you overwhelm your partner by addressing too many topics at once? **(yes or no)**
5. Do you interrupt while the speaker is speaking? **(yes or no)**
6. Do you ask 'why' questions? **(yes or no)**
7. Do you criticize what your partner thinks or does? **(yes or no)**
8. Do you attack your partner? **(yes or no)**
9. Do you attribute motives to your partner's behavior? **(yes or no)**
10. Do you defend yourself unnecessarily? **(yes or no)**

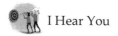

11. Do you minimize what your partner says? **(yes or no)**

12. Do you find yourself saying "you always..." or "you never..."? **(yes or no)**

13. Do you purposefully omit or perform actions in order to cause someone pain or discomfort? **(yes or no)**

If most of your answers are YES, then try to be more mindful of your words and actions and avoid these behaviors. They impede communication.

 I Hear You

PERSONAL EVALUATION OF YOUR COMMUNICATION

1. Do you go to the sender of the message to seek clarification regarding its intent? **(yes or no)**

2. Do you give your partner your full attention when he/she is speaking to you? **(yes or no)**

3. Do you listen with empathy and engage without contempt? **(yes or no)**

4. Do you ask your partner how he/she is feeling regarding the issue at hand? **(yes or no)**

5. Do you look your partner in the eye when you are spoken to? **(yes or no)**

6. Do you repeat your understanding of what you heard the speaker say? **(yes or no)**

7. When you disagree, do you ferret out the truth in your partner's position and admit that they are right? **(yes or no)**

8. Do you say, "you are right" when the speaker is right? **(yes or no)**

9. Do you say, "I forgive you"? **(yes or no)**

10. Do you say, "I am sorry" for the wrong doing? **(yes or no)**

11. Do you challenge your partner to forgive by asking, "Will you forgive me for the mistake **(Matthew 6:14)**?" **(yes or no)**

12. Do you stick to one subject at a time? **(yes or no)**.

13. Do you ask to be spoken to in a calmer, more respectful manner? **(yes or no)**

14. Do you set another time to get together and talk if you find you are unable to? **(yes or no)**

If most of your answers are NO, then try to be more mindful of your words and actions and avoid these behaviors. They impede communication.

 I Hear You

COMMUNICATION GROUND RULES

1. Before initiating dialogue, state objective first (the topic you want to discuss).

2. Ask questions to gather information about the topic to make sure that your impression of what happened regarding the matter is correct.

3. During discussion, evaluate conversation against stated objective.

4. Offer redirection if you believe the conversation has departed from the stated objective.

5. Stick to the communication model and keep feedback pertinent to the objective/subject of the message.

6. Do not tell the other person what he/she thinks or how he/she feels. Ask the question.

7. State what makes you anxious during conversation when you see it. Do not sit in silence or allow the disruptive emotion to overpower you.

 I Hear You

8. Give an explanation when it is asked for or when it is the objective of the conversation (trying to clarify the misperception).

9. Keep ground rules on hand for reference during conversation until they become familiar.

10. After conversation, the sender and receiver should evaluate his/her performance against points in debriefing tool. As pertinent, both parties offer feedback when each point is evaluated. Decode/debrief!

 I Hear You

DEFINITIONS

1. **Sender** – The person bringing the concern that is the topic of discussion. This is likely the offended party.

2. **Receiver** – The person to whom the concern being discussed is delivered; the person receiving the topic of discussion.

3. **Noise**- Any outside influence (physical, mental, or emotional) that has the potential to negatively impact the message.

4. **Insult** – An action or statement yielding a negative emotional impact.

5. **Shoveling** – Persistently questioning someone regarding a matter when he or she displays an unwillingness to freely give information; feeding someone words to describe the suspected emotion instead of waiting for it to be expressed.

6. **Clarifying Perception** – Deliberately asking a question of the offender in order to check if one's perception of an action or statement is true before reacting negatively to it.

7. **Rage** – A departure from the communication model that involves an angry escalation in tone of voice and body language.

8. **Shock Waving** – Introducing multiple topics during conversation in such a manner that the receiver is unable to address all the concerns voiced. (Topics should be introduced one at a time and thoroughly discussed before another is introduced.)

9. **Receiver-turned-Sender** – When the receiver receives a message and sends a message in response to it without giving feedback pertinent to the message received.

10. **Spitefulness** – Speaking words or performing an action with the intent of hurting another.

11. **Shut Down** – Intentionally or unintentionally withholding communication with the intent of negatively controlling or restricting the communication process.

12. **Attack** – Forcing one's perception of words or actions upon another without clarifying the intent of the original words or actions.

13. **Attributing False Motive** – Overriding someone's explained motive with one's own perception of his or her motivation.

14. **Devaluing Position** – Verbally refusing to give merit to another's position or feelings because they seem over-weighted or trivial.

15. **Challenging Forgiveness** – Verbally asking someone if the offense has been forgiven on their part.

16. **Failure** – The cessation of effort to move in the direction of achieving the set goal.

17. **Success** – Efforts /attempts leading to incremental steps away from negative communication patterns; moving in the direction of the goal until it is reached.

18. **Relapse** – This occurs when one departs from structured conversation and turns to previously established, negative communication styles.

19. **Verbal Abuse** – Speaking in an insulting manner to or about someone.

20. **Emotional Abuse** – Any act including confinement, isolation, verbal assault, humiliation, intimidation, or any other treatment which may diminish the sense of identity, dignity, and self-worth of an individual.

 I Hear You

DEBRIEFING INSTRUCTIONS

Debriefing is defined as quickly coming together to discuss identified barriers to a previous episode of communication and assigning healthy alternatives. This should be done as soon as possible using the debriefing record as a guide. Debriefing is done to unearth repetitive patterns of negative communication. It should be done after positively- as well as negatively-impacted conversations until the disruptive patterns are broken. See the debriefing record. The debriefing record is vital to identifying ingrained unhealthy behaviors.

The debriefing record is to be utilized as soon as possible after discussion has taken place regarding any issue that stirred emotions or needed clarification. It is used to evaluate the effectiveness and respectfulness of the communication that took place. It is to be done in a gentle, loving manner.

1. Sit together and replay the events of the conversation. Each person should have a sheet with his/her name on it.

2. It is important to establish who the sender was and who the receiver was so the responsibility

for each person can be assigned. When discussing segments of the conversation, identify whether you were the sender or the receiver by circling the "S" or "R" above that column on your debriefing record.

3. Place the date you are debriefing directly underneath the "R".

4. Take turns asking each other whether or not the elements in the column to the left were part of the communication. You will both ask the same question of each other for each category. Example: "Did I rage?" You will put Yes, No, or N/A in the box to the right of that element on the sheet immediately after the other person gives you the reply.

It is important to realize that not all categories in the debriefing tool will be seen in every interaction.

The response you place on your sheet will be the response given to you by the opposing party as it pertains to your performance or actions. It will be given to you by the person you were engaged with as it pertains to the topic on the debriefing sheet.

When debriefing, each party is looking at him or herself. We often do not see ourselves accurately, so we must trust the other person's opinion. After completing the entire column, it is advised that you revisit the information with the person whom you debriefed to gain insight into the areas where you need improvement. Explain to each other when and how you saw these elements. As you continue to debrief, periodically assess the sheet for areas where development is necessary. Approach this process with the attitude of self-discovery.

In order to avoid arguments, please do not challenge the other party on what they saw. Simply take the feedback and seek to improve in that area.

Debriefing should take no longer than 10 minutes to complete the entire column.

 I Hear You

DEBRIEFING RECORD

Focus On Behavior/Communication Only

Sender/ Receiver Date:	S R	S R	S R	S R	S R	S R	S R	S R	S R	S R	S R	S R	S R
Clarified Perception?													
Launched Attack?													
Spoke Calmly/Respectfully?													
Made Eye Contact?													
Over-Stated Feelings?													
Receiver-Turned-Sender?													
Shut Down?													
Raged/ Yelled?													
Defended													

 I Hear You

Shock Waved? (Too Many Topics)									
Interrupted Speaker Before Finished									
Criticized (Put Down)									
Avoided 'Why'									
Exhibited Unloving Behavior Change									
Attributed False Motive									
Devalued Position									
Apologized For Behavior /Speech									
Challenged Forgiveness									

 I Hear You

FEELING WORDS

Page Instructions

If you have trouble finding the right word to express your feelings, please use this page to assist you. Many individuals are reared in households where they were not encouraged to explore and identify what feeling is causing the upset. The lack of practice can make this transition difficult. Refer to this page prior to initiating conversations that express what you are feeling. Use it to help identify what emotion you are feeling then express it.

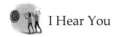 I Hear You

EXAMPLES OF FEELING WORDS

GLAD	SAD	MAD	AFRAID
content	blah	bugged	uncomfortable
glad	blue	annoyed	startled
pleased	gloomy	irritated	uneasy
playful	rotten	mean	tense
cheerful	sad	crabby	anxious
giddy	unhappy	cranky	worried
comfortable	empty	grumpy	concerned
cozy	********	grouchy	timid
safe		********	*********
relaxed	*********		
confident	disappointed	*********	*********
strong	hurt	disgusted	
peaceful	lost	ticked off	alarmed
********	sorry	mad	scared
delighted	ashamed	angry	afraid
jolly	lonely	smoldering	frightened
bubbly	down	hot	fearful
tickled	hopeless	frustrated	threatened
silly	discouraged	impatient	trembled
frisky	awful		shaken
happy	**********	*********	disturbed

31

 I Hear You

proud			********
joyful	**********	*********	
excited	unloved	fed-up	********
thankful	wounded	fuming	dreading
great	miserable	infuriated	panicky
loved	crushed	destructive	terrified
loving	helpless	explosive	horrified
blissful	depressed	violent	petrified
grateful	withdrawn	enraged	
satisfied	heartbroken	furious	
********			
alive			
sparky			
wonderful			
ecstatic			
terrific			
jubilant			

 I Hear You

CASE STUDY INSTRUCTIONS

Throughout this book are several case studies. They are there to help make application of what you understand about the pitfalls of ineffective communication. As you read the case study, give thought to what you are told about each personality. Analyze the action each character in the study takes during the interaction. The studies are not gender-specific. Please place your focus on the behaviors and what led to them. There may not necessarily be a right or wrong answer; however, there is usually a healthier choice that could have been made to protect the relationships in the studies. The case studies are taken from true circumstances and have been embellished to highlight the impact of ineffective communication and the hurt that yields these communication patterns. Have fun as you apply your knowledge to these cases.

COMMUNICATION GOALS

GOALS:

1. To strengthen communication between parties in order to avoid the negative cycles that strain relationships and the hurt that blocks effective communication.

2. To decode routine conversations occurring between parties with the aim of identifying and eliminating filters and behaviors that impact the process negatively.

3. To replace negative filters and behaviors with healthy, respectful alternatives.

COMMITMENT:

1. To practice using the communication model moving forward, with a focus on perfecting the usage of its content by debriefing until it is fluent and serves as a natural replacement for the existing, poorly-functioning form of communication.

2. To be willing to depart from taking a right vs. wrong position and place the focus on honest communication that has the objective of hearing the intended message and trying to gain an understanding of the feelings that support the message.

James 1: 19-20 reminds every person to "…be quick to listen, slow to speak and slow to become angry, because human anger does not produce the righteousness that God desires."

FOUNDATIONAL PRINCIPLE (*CORE CONCEPT*)

The sum of life's experiences can cause individuals to develop sensitivities, which in turn leads to the development of filters that impact hearing. These filters can disrupt hearing, causing people who hear the same set of words to process the meaning of those words differently.

 I Hear You

Each individual therefore is charged with the responsibility of confirming the meaning of words heard before reacting to them.

"The tongue of the wise adorns knowledge, but the mouth of the fool gushes folly." **(Prov. 15:2)**

 I Hear You

EXPRESSIONS OF FEELING

Which of the following statements properly express the sender's feelings?

Please read each sentence below as if you are the sender of the message. If you believe the statement expresses what the sender is feeling please circle **Yes**, if not then circle **No**. (See answers in Appendix A.)

1. Why do you always make that face when I ask you a question? **(Yes No)**
2. I feel like you don't care about anyone but yourself. **(Yes No)**
3. I feel emotionally deprived right now. **(Yes No)**
4. It was belittling to be treated that way. **(Yes No)**
5. I feel like you were rude at the dinner table tonight. **(Yes No)**
6. Why don't you ever say you love me? **(Yes No)**
7. It would warm my heart right now to hear you say you love me. **(Yes No)**
8. When you make that face, I feel anxious because I think I've done something wrong. **(Yes No)**

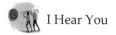 I Hear You

9. That gets on my last nerve. I hate it when you do that. **(Yes No)**

10. It annoyed me when you repeatedly asked that question. **(Yes No)**

11. It hurt to be spoken to that way in front of our guests. **(Yes No)**

 I Hear You

THE KEY TO EMOTIONAL HEALING
(Lighting the Path)

Each person is responsible for clearly and effectively conveying the feelings that he or she possesses.

When a statement of feeling is properly made, it places ownership of the emotion on the sender or owner of the feeling.

It states the sender's perception of the catalyst that generated the feeling. It correctly states, "I felt...

when that happened." It avoids accusations such as, "<u>You</u> made me feel... when <u>you</u>...." When the receiver hears the message, the focus of the reply should be placed on the sender's expressed emotion. The reply should attempt to soothe or calm. The receiver is less likely to offer a defense if he or she is not accused. One should not defend against what someone is feeling because the feeling is neither right nor wrong. Doing so offers no consideration to the feeling that was expressed. The defense places the focus on the receiver instead of addressing the need of the sender. This action makes the receiver a poor listener.

The expression is merely an exposure of the sender's current emotional state. Sharing what we feel is an expression of trust. Our loved ones are drawn to us when we demonstrate our trust and confidence in them. They will likely be hurt when they discover that we do not trust them.

The inability to properly and respectfully express what one is feeling, coupled with the expectation that the receiver should understand what one is feeling based on an ineffective message is a pitfall.

It repeatedly places undue stress on the relationship.

It is unfair and unreasonable to expect someone else to know one's feelings without expressing them. In **Psalm 119:105** the bible states, "Your word is a lamp for my feet, a light on my path." If we are to convey an effective message regarding our emotional state, we must speak the words. Relying on someone to shovel away by repeatedly questioning in an effort to uncover our hidden feelings will hinder our development. It is also frustrating, since the task can be quite arduous. Understanding this makes it more imperative that one allows time for personal development in this area of communication.

Once feelings are expressed, they become a roadmap for the receiver, lighting the path to the proper action for the receiver to take in order to offer comfort and soothing.

The inverse of this is also true. The lack of expressed feeling yields darkness and confusion to the receiver who is sincerely willing and anxiously seeking the path to corrective action. When someone notices through a nonverbal display that something has changed and he or she makes an inquiry about the change, the inferred question is, "Will you please let me in?" Taking action that closes this individual out is a rejection and a denial of intimacy. When offered emotional support by our loved one, we ought to open the doors to our heart widely and take the time to release the feelings respectfully, thereby letting that person in so he or she can offer loving comfort. Continued refusal is likened to building a wall that over time will prove difficult to scale.

The delayed release of information pertaining to the feelings will prolong and intensify the hurt of the sender. As the validation or clarification of the words or action that awakened the feelings remains unavailable, the sender has a tendency to revisit the hurt thereby stacking or compressing it. It should now be obvious that the sender who is incapable, unwilling, or afraid to expose the aroused feelings is basically shooting oneself in the foot. The expression of the feelings is the metaphorical key that unlocks the door to healthy, healing communication. The inability or unwillingness to express feelings is a flagrant injustice to self.

The person for whom expressing feelings does not come easily should routinely take personal time to practice stating messages. These messages should clearly indicate what we are feeling. The supplied list of feeling words will help with that effort. With practice, one will soon find it becomes easier to do so. Those within close proximity to this person may be accustomed to coaching this individual through the act of expressing feelings. While this action is viewed as a survival mechanism by those performing it, it is actually dysfunctional, because it provides the support necessary to allow the emotionally suppressed individual to remain in a position of unhealthy complacency. However, it is not uncommon for this person to resist this form of coaching once emotional development begins to accelerate in this area of communication. This is a healthy response that requires those supportive individuals to step back and allow this individual to perform the necessary self-expression, which will ultimately yield emotional growth and healing. This emotional growth allows relationships to thrive as the healthy expression decreases stress and improves the self-esteem of the host.

It is worth stating here that shoveling to uncover feelings for an individual, then stating them for that person to agree or disagree with may be done out of love, but is unhealthy. Healthy support involves self-discovery and self-expression, thereby eliminating the dependency.

When a message is sent, there is always the potential for it to be misinterpreted. When misinterpreted and not clarified, the offended receiver may respond in a hurtful manner. The reply may cause the sender to be emotionally wounded. In view of the fact that hurt causes one to focus on self, there is the potential for a scenario in which no one will have their hurt addressed. Once hurt, both parties will have emotional needs.

Respectfully expressing one's hurt without delivering a hurtful blow is key to avoiding this negative cycle.

CHALLENGE

Please take a few minutes to sit down with your loved one and ask, "Do we see any of the above content in our relationship?" If so, "What action can we take to improve in this area?"

It is important to take time to perform tasks that guard and protect our bond in relationships. Routinely looking at the functionality of one's communication and seeking to strengthen it is one sure way to achieve that goal.

 I Hear You

CASE STUDY (THE DINNER INVITATION)

Dwayne is leaving work late and is tired. Before exiting, his coworker, Priscilla, invites him and his wife to a gathering for dinner. His wife, Susan, has been home all day and spent the greater part of the day running errands and attending to their children. When Dwayne arrives home, he makes no mention of the invitation to Susan. He greets her then retreats to their bedroom for about 10 minutes. He then goes into the hall bathroom and begins washing his hands. While Dwayne is washing his hands, the phone rings and Susan answers. It is Priscilla, Dwayne's coworker, asking if they plan to come to dinner. After a brief exchange, Susan hangs up. Dwayne comes out of the bathroom and asks Susan, "What's for dinner?" She glares at him with a fallen countenance. "Were you planning to tell me about the dinner invitation?" Dwayne is initially silent then says, "Oh yeah, it slipped my mind. I didn't think you wanted to be around those people anyway." Susan becomes flushed. "You are so inconsiderate and selfish!" she exclaims. "It is so rude of you to just make the decision to stay home without consulting me." She walks into the kitchen and removes a can of tuna from the cupboard.

 I Hear You

"Tuna," she replies. "We're having tuna." Dwayne remains silent.

(See commentary in Appendix C.)

QUESTIONS (Write yours answers on a separate sheet of paper.)

1. What went wrong during this exchange?
2. Based on her statements, what do you think Susan was feeling?
3. Do you think she was effective in telling Dwayne how she was feeling?
4. How could she have worded her message to be more effective in conveying her feelings?
5. Could Dwayne have chosen a better response to her message?
6. Did either party hurt the other?

 I Hear You

HOW DO I LOVE ME? (*Protecting our Self-Esteem and Self-Image*)

As aforementioned, there are situations and conditions under which we are reared that can have a direct impact on the manner in which we maneuver ourselves. While it is unhealthy to be so self-absorbed that one develops an inability to be empathic, it is extremely important that one routinely takes time to learn and understand which actions need to be taken to maintain and develop a healthy self-esteem and self-image.

Some of us were reared under the supervision of parents who were remiss regarding creating a healthy environment that allows the self-esteem and self-image of their children to flourish. Making the choice to express feelings and views as well as facilitating that expression is vital. Allow yourself and others to make choices and be responsible for the consequences of the decisions. This process facilitates cognitive maturity. It enhances our development as well as understanding of needs as they pertain to self. One who understands self is better able to communicate needs, thereby equipping others to better relate to him or her. **Proverbs 27:17** reminds us, "As iron sharpens iron, so one person sharpens another."

An individual who fails to develop the skill of being introspective can sometimes find him or herself in crisis when struck by the realization that he or she does not have a firm grasp on identifying personal wants or needs. When involved in an interpersonal relationship, this void in personal development can cause conflict and confusion.

When attempts to express needs and opinions pertaining to self lead to conflict, some individuals may choose to eliminate the conflict by acquiescing

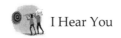

to the position of another. What is this behavior called? It is referred to as people-pleasing. Years of making this choice can lead to feelings of oppression. It can also cause one to feel devalued. When entrenched in this pattern, it is likely that one's self-esteem and self-image will suffer. This repeated action can lead to the pattern of blaming others who more readily express themselves, for your personal choice to be silent.

When involved in a close personal relationship with someone who freely expresses feelings and desires, this reserved individual, who "goes with the flow", can develop feelings of resentment towards the person who is very sure of self and quickly offers input. The reservation and lack of practice in the areas of evaluation and decision-making associated with the chosen life of silence will ultimately lead to frustration. This cycle of frustration yields feelings of inadequacy, which in turn causes this individual to be more willing to go with the decisions offered by another.

People-pleasing behavior will ensure that one is not heard. It will also solidify the belief that others do not care about what one wants or feels.

These feelings can intensify and manifest themselves in the form of negative behavior directed at others who are in close relationships with this individual. This pattern of behavior is not only unhealthy; it tears at the bonds holding the relationship and weakens the foundation.

Chronically choosing to be silent when one should express one's opinion and make choices is a pitfall.

Strengthen your self-esteem and self-image. Let your opinion and preferences be known.

 I Hear You

TEST 1

(Answers in Appendix B)

1. What type of interactions do we debrief?

2. When a statement of feeling is properly made, it places ownership of the emotion on the _____ or owner of the _____.

3. When someone expresses a feeling, what are two things the receiver is expected to do?
   a. Give _____ pertaining to the _____.

   b. Address the _____ heard.

4. What does expressing the feeling without making an accusation do for the receiver?

5. Why is shoveling to uncover the feelings of someone reluctant to share them contraindicated? What should we do instead?

 I Hear You

6. When communicating, why are we encouraged not to rage or display threatening behaviors?

7. The absence of communication or its delay is equal to or worse than ineffective communication because it allows issues to _____, which leads to other _____.

8. Other than conveying information, the primary goal of communication should be to avoid or _____ _____.

9. What is one's negative reaction to a present action or statement usually tied to?

10. According to the foundational principle of our communication model, each individual is charged with the responsibility of confirming the meaning of _____ before _____ to them.

 I Hear You

MODEL 1: EFFECTIVE COMMUNICATION

Notice that the communication channels in the model are clear. Clearing the communication channels of noise will increase efficacy during the process.

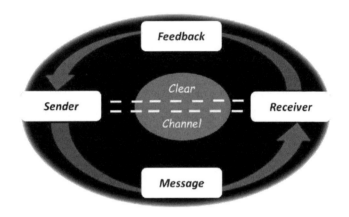

COMPONENTS OF CLEAR COMMUNICATION

1. **Sender** – The owner of the message being discussed.

2. **Message** – The information conveyed via verbal or nonverbal stimuli.

3. **A Clear Channel** – The unimpeded path through which the message travels.

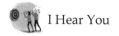 I Hear You

4. **Receiver** – The recipient of the verbal or nonverbal message.

5. **Feedback** – The verbal or nonverbal reply pertaining to the content of the received message.

As aforestated, when conveying information, messages should be formulated to deliver concise thoughts and should therefore be worded carefully to accomplish that goal. When conversation begins, both parties are to bring their focus to the sender's message. It is important that the sender pauses after delivering the message to give the receiver an opportunity to offer feedback pertaining to the message received. Take note that I did not say "messages". The sender should avoid sending other messages before getting feedback to the initial message. In view of the fact that people tend to respond quickly to the last message heard, other messages should be contained until the primary message is addressed. Unloading multiple messages or "shock waving" the receiver is a pitfall.

In order to remain focused on the message, comments regarding the process that are not intended to bring clarification to the message should be temporarily held then discussed during

 I Hear You

the debriefing session. This action helps in keeping the focus on the message.

MODEL 2: INEFFECTIVE COMMUNICATION

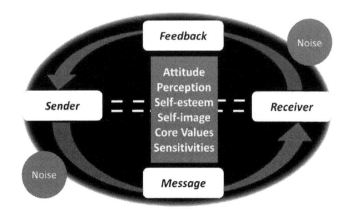

Note the filters and noise that hinder communication.

It is unhealthy to expect someone to sit and absorb multiple messages without first gaining an understanding of the initial one received. Doing so will ultimately lead to misunderstandings. If the receiver does not respond to a message after it is sent, it is usually an indicator that something is not quite right.

In order to facilitate healthy communication, it is important for the sender to realize that it is important to wait for a reply to the initial message

 I Hear You

once it is introduced. Chronic failure of the receiver to address messages will lead to frustration and conflict. The receiver should avoid giving any feedback until he or she has given feedback that addresses the initial message received. One should remain cognizant of the process and his or her current role in it.

The only focus of the receiver should be to gain an understanding of the message then issue feedback that lovingly addresses the feeling or concern.

If the initial message was sent for the purpose of giving information, the receiver should respond by expressing understanding of the information received. If the receiver responds by becoming a sender, the process will immediately breakdown.

Example: Terri and Troy, a married couple.

Terri: Hey, Troy, can I speak with you for a minute?

Troy: Sure. What's on your mind?

Terri: I just noticed that during the worship service you appeared to be spending increasingly more time on your phone. This morning I noticed several people glancing over at you at different times when you were scrolling through it and the minister was preaching. I felt a little embarrassed, but didn't think that was the time to address it.

Troy [the wrong reply]: You always have something to say about what I'm doing. Why are you always playing the victim? Can I ever have a peaceful moment? How do they know what I'm doing on my phone…?

Troy [the correct reply]: I'm so sorry if my actions caused you embarrassment. It wasn't my intention. I can see how that looks. Please forgive me for not catching that.

Proverbs 18:13 states, "To answer before listening — that is folly and shame." When responding as a defensive receiver, the individual will likely reply with hurtful remarks. In this instance, the sender of the original message will likely feel disrespected, insulted, and hurt. This reaction subjects the sender who trustingly expressed an initial message of personal pain, to the verbal attack of the angry receiver who failed to clarify the message, personalized it as an attack, and then replied with hurtful words. This sequence of actions usually occurs swiftly, and will compound the sender's existing hurt. The angry receiver is then viewed as not only hurtful, but also inconsiderate and insensitive. It goes without stating that someone stuck in this cycle has a limited capacity to love. People who have been exposed to unexplained, angry attacks for extended periods can unwittingly function from a defensive position. This defensive posture can cause them to inflict the same type of hurt, thus completing the cycle of hurt people hurting others. After years of being in a defensive position, it is possible for one to demonstrate less and less remorse for the actions that inflict hurt upon others. It is for these reasons that people who have been in a relationship for years will sometimes suddenly decide to exit it. The pain simply becomes too great.

In some cases, the person who readily mounts a defense without clearly hearing the message and clarifying it is likely experiencing some degree of anxiety. This emotion obscures information, and when confronted this individual will likely see it as an attack regardless of the presentation. Most will not recognize the gradual hardening of the heart, since he or she sees him or herself as being under attack. If one discovers that he or she is in the

 I Hear You

position of the angry receiver, the corrective action should be to quickly admit one's fault and issue an apology to the recipient of the hurtful, defensive attacks.

Failing to take responsibility for the hurt for which we *are* responsible is a pitfall.

Responding this way chronically will tax one's support system, which may cause some to withdraw due to the stress. In view of the fact that we often do not see ourselves, one should take heed when repeatedly informed of one's defensive posture. As stated previously in the section entitled "Lighting the Path", it is important to properly express one's feelings if we want the receiver to be able to identify and respond appropriately to our needs.

An angry, defensive response to stated feelings is unhealthy and is suggestive of other issues that need to be addressed.

 I Hear You

      Insensitive   **Sensitive**

Choose Which You Would Like To Be.

Understanding one's role during the process also helps to identify where to intervene and offer guidance that facilitates adherence to the process. The sender who is focused on the message will take time to ensure its clarity. The focused receiver will readily seek clarification to ensure that the correct message was received. Without proper understanding, the receiver will likely be lost in regard to what the proper composition of the feedback should be. The receiver's failure to issue proper feedback is usually due to a selfish focus.

 I Hear You

Once basic physiological needs are met, one of the most significant needs of humans is to be heard.

Taking time to listen to the sender and then giving feedback conveys respect.

It also completes the communication cycle. Refusing to listen to the concerns of one's significant other will lead to the compressing of feelings and subsequent emotional explosions. Healthy communication requires loving consideration, sensitivity, respect, and skill. **Proverbs 15:1** tells us "A gentle answer turns away wrath, but a harsh word stirs up anger."

CHALLENGE

The next time you engage in conversation, try to identify whether or not you can determine what your role is and how well you remain in the proper role during the conversation. During conversation, it is healthy for roles to naturally shift to and fro while adhering to the topic of discussion. However, we must be careful to address one message before introducing another. Remaining in the position of sender in a relationship forces the other party to be a sponge, which is unhealthy.

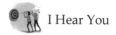 I Hear You

TRUST THE PROCESS *(How Does It Flow?)*

When considering the flow of communication, it is important to first realize that communication is typically imperfect. Embracing the nature of this imperfect process makes it more reasonable to set a goal of learning how to navigate through it effectively. In order to do this, it is imperative that we understand the model, the position we occupy, and our responsibility while in that position. The following serves as a general guide regarding the flow of conversation. Please reference Model 2 before you begin reading this module.

The sender requests time to have a discussion (the other party becomes the receiver).

The receiver responds by stating availability and then states readiness when the time arrives.

In order to expedite resolution, the receiver should be limited to one day to issue a response to the request. The longer we wait, the greater the misperceptions become. The longer we wait, the harder one's heart becomes.

Any allotted time greater than one day should be mutually agreed upon. If any party fails to remember the details of the discussion during debriefing, it is recommended that the interval between insult and debriefing be shortened.

If applicable, the sender states the message in terms of feeling hurt, disrespected, offended, or feeling unloved based on a perceived verbal or nonverbal message **(See Ephesians 5: 25-33).**

The receiver responds by clarifying the message heard and if found inaccurate by the sender, the message is repeatedly clarified by the sender until the receiver is able to state the message accurately. It is not permitted to attempt to replace the sender's message with your perception of the message. The receiver's primary role at this point is to listen to the message in order to identify where the hurt occurred in an effort to remove it. If the sender states, "That is not the message I sent," the response should be one that facilitates clarification of the message. "Will you please state your message again?" Or "I don't understand what it is you are feeling. Will you please use a feeling word?"

If parties reach an impasse, then it is helpful for another party to be called in to assist with decoding/debriefing. Decoding/debriefing adheres to communication rules and is an objective process. Do not try to bend the principles to suit your desires.

 I Hear You

THE NEGATIVE IMPACT OF ANXIETY ON COMMUNICATION

As stated in the discussion of Model 2 (Ineffective Communication), an angry, defensive response to stated feelings is unhealthy and is suggestive of other issues that need to be addressed. One such issue is anxiety. It is important for the person who becomes anxious during communication to realize the negative impact that this emotion can have. Some anxious individuals are often very defensive and have the propensity to say and do very hurtful things.

Most individuals who become anxious when it is necessary to confront someone and communicate will begin negative self-talk as soon as they become aware that serious conversation is necessary. They often feel a sense of having done something wrong before conversation ensues. This creates a defensive posture. This negative self-talk becomes almost ritualistic in nature and will impede communication before it begins. The host of these emotions will become visibly charged as the preparation for battle begins. Once words are spoken, this defensive receiver is looking for blame and will often skew the message to support that quest. Often, physiological signs such as posturing, eyes widening, and a change in facial expression can be seen. These signs should not be present before conversation begins, nor should they be present if the conversation is not threatening. This ritual prepares the mind of the anxious person to process the interaction as an attack, thus making the prediction a reality.

The sender entangled in conversation with this person will quickly begin to clarify and restate messages, but once in battle mode, this entrenched defensive receiver will be unable to hear the redirection or clarification. When overwhelmed with self-induced tension, this person will obviously be a poor receiver/listener. This receiver will almost immediately become a sender before ever addressing the content of the message received. The person prone to anxiety has an extreme need to clarify messages due to this tendency but usually does not, due to the lack of awareness. The disruption of the process by the presence of two senders will yield frustration for both parties, which is often an end product of an attempt to communicate with this individual. It goes without stating that someone stuck in this cycle has a limited capacity to love due to the hurt inflicted on others from the fear of being hurt by spoken words. The question worth asking:

"Is someone who is making themselves vulnerable to you by expressing their feelings during their quest for comfort trying to hurt you? Is the use of this defensive, hurtful shield necessary?"

First John 4:18 states, "There is no fear in love. But perfect love drives out fear, because fear has to do with punishment. The one who fears is not made perfect in love."

Anxiety causes a high degree of misunderstanding during communication.

The anxious communicator will not only skew information, but will likely perform with a high degree of error and misunderstanding due to their defensive, emotional position.

At times, the replies to messages from this person may be completely off-topic and seem irrational. It is not uncommon for the stress of the anxiety to cause forgetfulness, which leads to embarrassment. Over time, this emotion may begin to influence the individual's self-esteem and create an overwhelming desire to be right. This desire, stemming from developmentally early repeated attacks, can lead to the twisting of information to accomplish that goal. This changing of information during conversation adds confusion and frustration to the process, which is a result of the mixed messages.

The focus of the anxious communicator is disrupted, which makes it difficult to concentrate. The inability to concentrate presents a challenge when trying to adhere to a respectful, structured process. Burdened with emotion, it then becomes difficult to clarify the message, identify which role he or she is currently occupying, and then give an appropriate, pertinent response. This defensive individual will very seldom be able to identify and address the emotional needs of the sender due to the defensive posture and the personal need for emotional soothing. It soon becomes clear that this receiver is more focused on protecting self than responding appropriately to the message. Once away from the immediate threat, the desperate need for emotional survival no longer exists. Therefore, the defensive shield should be laid to rest.

This process is usually very deeply seated and likely stems from this person being repeatedly subjected to verbal assaults by a sender or senders during formative or later years. This experience produces emotional pain, which yields a defensive response. Years of performing this defensive ritual yields a deeply-seated defensive position that becomes second nature to the host. Though he or she may feel like a victim, the recipient of this abuse eventually becomes an attacker, as well. This transformation completes the cycle of a victim maturing into an attacker. When this individual leaves the environment in which the attacking began, this deeply-seated, second-natured response goes with him or her. Over time, the cycle is repeated indefinitely unless it is brought to awareness. Again I ask, "Is the use of this defensive, hurtful shield necessary?"

Anxiety related to communication is very disruptive and must therefore be addressed before healthy communication will begin to thrive.

The mechanism given by God for the building of emotional intimacy—loving communication—can remain arrested until the anxiety is properly addressed.

It is possible to reverse this process, but it requires time and patience. Some cases may need professional help. The host of this behavior must first be willing to own it. Most often, the host of this anxiety is unaware and finds it easier to blame his or her response on the approach of the sender or words used to convey the message. If the sender is not angrily attacking, one who is not anxious will usually be able to receive a message, clarify it if necessary, and then give an appropriate, pertinent response.

 I Hear You

WHO AM I? (UNDERSTANDING YOUR PERSONALITY TYPE)

When it comes to making changes in the manner in which we communicate, it is helpful to understand our own personality type before deciding which areas need to be improved. Whether you are the sender or the receiver, one must exercise self-control in order to become an effective communicator. The receiver must eliminate all noise (as seen in Model 2) and listen carefully with the intent of identifying and addressing the hurt. The sender must take time to consider the delivery of the message in order to avoid hurting. Remember that messages are both verbal and nonverbal. It is important to realize that the goal of recognizing the personalities below is to bring to the forefront of our mind the dysfunction that rests with the unhealthy ones and thereby limit the time we spend occupying those positions.

 I Hear You

THE ATTACKER

The attacker is usually a poor listener who believes the contrary. This person is defensive and easily angered. When confronted, this person may feel blamed regardless of the approach. The attacker very easily distorts both verbal and visual information and tends to be egocentric.

Ironically, this lack of objectivity causes this person to feel like a victim when in fact he or she is the aggressor.

 I Hear You

When asked to sit and communicate, this person will feel as if he or she has done something wrong before conversation ensues, triggering a defensive posture. The attacker will accuse and blame, before or without asking questions. The single most effective tool one can utilize to remain out of the position of the attacker is to ask a clarifying question when someone says or does something with which you disagree.

The attacker acts mostly out of emotion and the primary emotion displayed by the attacker is anger. Thoughts coming from this sender are usually premeditated, many times erroneous, and usually expressed negatively. Anger is the usual conduit used for the attacker's delivery of a message. An attacker will have difficulty hearing the intended message sent because he is caught up in his feelings before a word is spoken or quickly thereafter. This action makes the attacker a poor listener. Most attackers tend to personalize issues then take time to engage in defensive premeditation. It is during this time that the **heart begins to harden** and the negative position takes root. In order to avoid this behavior, we must understand how hurtful it is to force this negative view upon someone. By asking clarifying questions, we retrain our behavior in a manner that allows us to incorporate the input of others into our thoughts before we solidify them. This is a powerful demonstration of respect for the other individual. The contrary is also true. It is a powerful act of disrespect to formulate negative pictures of someone without asking questions first.

The attacker usually has difficulty expressing emotions in terms of feeling words and may try to express feelings by discussing events that precipitated his or her anger. Attackers use their attack as a defense and seldom ask clarifying questions or return understanding of the message received. This action further builds upon the previous misperception. The attacker is rooted in his position due to premeditation without investigation and seeks to get the receiver to see his position before trying to gain understanding. He or she fully believes the negative picture that has been painted so innocently. The receiver in communication with this individual will find him or herself explaining and trying desperately to clarify misperceptions. The attacker may become frustrated and view the receiver as not taking accountability when the source of contention is his own misperception. Always try to understand the *why* behind someone's words or actions before

solidifying your position and pushing your perception forward.

The attacker may exhibit varying degrees of spitefulness. This spitefulness is easily acted upon after the negative image formed from sensitivity has been painted. In the face of conflict, the attacker will be shielded. He or she will refuse to engage you in conversation due to bitterness, and emerges only to further accuse based on their misperceptions. It is best to emerge to gain understanding by asking questions. Communication with this individual is very difficult. Attackers may see themselves as victims, but they truly are not.

 I Hear You

THE SPONGE

The sponge will usually choose to absorb the unfair treatment of others despite feeling mistreated themselves. This person is full of compressed emotions and chooses not to express them because he or she "does not wish to argue". The sponge may have difficulty putting feelings into words since he or she is not in the practice of doing so and chooses to be inappropriately silent. This person is also full of misperceptions due to his or her reluctance to communicate when there is a need to confront someone. Some may find the sponge to be closed and withdrawn, which can lead to feelings of frustration due to difficulty connecting with this person. When the sponge chooses to communicate,

 I Hear You

the approach will be much like the attacker—done in anger and without attempting to clarify the message received. It is an explosion precipitated by stored and compressed emotions. Having spoken, the sponge is usually not heard due to the focus placed on the sudden change in behavior.

THE OSTRICH

The ostrich openly admits to disliking confrontation and will purposefully try to avoid it. Therefore, the ostrich is uncomfortable with face-to-face conflict resolution. The ostrich displays a concern for being liked by others and usually goes with the flow. This behavior can sometimes generate mistrust. The ostrich will sometimes speak

in generalities in instances where he or she should be very pointed. When communicating with the ostrich, the receiver will sometimes be unaware that he or she is the focus of the conversation and will miss the message, thereby missing information that could be good, constructive criticism. Misperceptions are also common to this person due to the reluctance to confront. The ostrich is often reluctant to use sentences that disclose their feelings. There is a tendency to tell white lies in order to avoid confrontation. Taking the position of an ostrich will sometimes cause the loss of respect from others. The ostrich may tend to be a Road Runner (see below) at times, because they do not want to be held accountable for their involvement in a matter.

KEY POINT

Sending indirect messages benefits only the sender who walks away believing that he or she was able to deliver the message **safely**. The receiver will seldom make application of the message in a meaningful way. Indirect messages are at best ineffective. Some may see this form of communication as disrespectful and are offended by it.

 I Hear You

THE ROAD RUNNER

The Road Runner is also a person who is uncomfortable with confrontation and will go to great lengths to avoid it. The list of excuses given by this individual for not coming together to discuss an issue can be extensive. The most common are: I don't feel well. Something hurts. I'm not up to it right now. None of these excuses will be followed by a set date to have the needed conversation.

 I Hear You

The road runner brings information from one party to the next without the goal of bringing the two parties together and can therefore be intentionally or unintentionally divisive. People caught up in unhealthy patterns of communication will take information brought by the road runner and utilize it to harden their heart. One must avoid presenting information that can be misconstrued. We must always get the information from the original source. Exercise caution when running between parties and delivering information. This action can cause greater strain upon the already injured relationship. Make all attempts to bring the parties together for face-to-face discussion.

The road runner tends to make emotional decisions and is therefore prone to making mistakes. The actions of this person may cause others to lose respect. He is prone to making false impressions. Communication with the road runner is often very deceptive.

 I Hear You

THE DIPLOMAT

The diplomat enjoys the presence of others and eagerly engages in conversation. He or she is usually seen as confident. The diplomat will seek conflict resolution quickly, and effectively solves problems. The diplomat is typically a firm personality and governs himself with strong opinions based on a factual source rather than emotion. People who do not understand this personality will tend to think this person wants to be right, but in truth this person wants to be factual

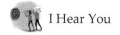 I Hear You

and accurate. He is very comfortable making mistakes since they are simply learning opportunities. This person sends very pointed messages and prefers face-to-face communication. Before making a decision, the diplomat will ask multiple questions to ensure that his vision is accurate and to avoid causing injury to others. He craves information regarding the issue at hand. Seen as outgoing, the diplomat is alert to the people around him and seems to have never met a stranger. He adapts quickly. The diplomat is a listener and will research information with any degree of novelty to it. Diplomats share information readily and can seem opinionated because of that. This person will stand up for others and himself quite comfortably. He is intolerant of what he sees as unfair or disrespectful. Communication with this person is usually clear and pointed.

KEY POINT

If you find yourself in a position where you have multiple strained relationships, ask yourself: "Am I taking the time to go to people and ask them clarifying questions? Am I making assumptions, dwelling on them, and then accusing someone

about a misperception that I have not discussed with the source of the original message?" If you find that people tend to explain things to you and you do not understand why, you may be unintentionally accusing them of things they have not done or positions they have not taken. You may need to evaluate whether you are effectively stating what happened and how it made you feel when you approach them. That is simply all the information someone needs in order to address the hurt feeling.

 I Hear You

WHOSE MESSAGE IS IT? *(WHO HAS THE RIGHT TO DEFINE IT?)*

The message is the property of the sender. All effort must be made by the receiver to understand the message received. The focus of all conversation should be on the sender's message. The receiver must exert all effort to avoid turning the focus of the conversation onto self. Failing to immediately address the message heard will likely lead to conflict since the pain or issue of concern will remain unaddressed.

The receiver's concern for the message displays empathy. If there is dispute over the message, only the sender/owner of the message has the right to clarify it. We should not adamantly tell the sender what he or she said. It is very possible for the understanding of the spoken words to differ from the sender's intended meaning.

Redefining the message then forcing one's perception of the message onto its sender is a pitfall. It will usually lead to conflict.

Avoid engaging in conversation that chases a misunderstanding of the message unless it is simply to acknowledge the misperception itself. It is most effective for the receiver to state to the sender what message was heard. This action allows for clarification and eliminates unnecessary conflict.

We must also avoid walking away from a conversation then changing the meaning of the message into one that fits more in line with our mistrust or preconceived ideas.

In order to avoid distorting messages, all effort must be made to:

1. Listen to the sender and adhere to the content of the message.

2. Return understanding once the sender is finished speaking.

3. Address the feelings expressed by the sender before any other discussion begins.

It is best for the sender to initially state only the feelings caused by the event, then pause for the receiver's reply.

There is a difference between defending oneself and clarifying a misperception. In these instances there is always the intended message and the misperception. The person who is seeking clarification will ask a question to clarify their perception. Asking clarifying questions should not be viewed as a defense. The receiver may clearly understand that the feelings of the sender were generated by something he or she said or did and accepts that responsibility. When confronted, it is best for the receiver to quickly address the feeling of hurt, and then clarify the sender's misperception of the verbal or nonverbal message.

The person who instinctively attacks tends to generate intense feelings quickly due to personal sensitivities. When motivated by emotion, the person offering a defense will quickly overlook the message he or she received. Once a misperception is formulated, it is easy to find other actions that seem to bolster the misunderstanding. This person may find it easier to wait until something else looks supportive of the misperception, then approach the receiver with false assurance. The problem with this approach is that without seeking clarification first, the action simply solidifies his or her misperception. Doing so is an aggressive move and a request for conflict.

Addressing someone in this manner usually leads to the offering of the facts that should have been sought previously. It is unhealthy for someone to remain silent (be a sponge) and absorb the accusation of someone who is hurt by his or her assumption or misperception.

 I Hear You

WHO DID IT? (WHO IS RESPONSIBLE?)

When the driver of an automobile loses control of it and the vehicle collides with another vehicle, which in turn strikes another, and yet another, the responsibility for the series of accidents is placed on the driver of the vehicle initiating the first collision. The responsible party will be asked to provide reparation. Likewise, when we lose control of ourselves and deliver the initial insult that becomes the precipitator to a series of negative events, the responsibility for the situation at large is

placed on the owner of that initial insult. That person must quickly take action to prevent a single insult from becoming a series of negative events. Regardless of the position we play—sender or receiver—we all have a responsibility in the communication cycle. The more quickly we claim that responsibility, the more fluent communication becomes. If we are to have healthy relationships, we must be willing to assume responsibility for our actions and words that cause others perceived emotional pain when they are brought to our attention.

Each party must take the role of willing participant in identifying negative cycles that are specific to the relationship and be willing to offer what he or she sees as a viable solution in breaking that particular cycle. If not, one party will likely begin to feel dominated by the other. Sitting in silence or leaving the work of finding solutions for one party to perform can have the potential to cause a negative tilt.

James 4:17 tells us, "If anyone, then, knows the good they ought to do and doesn't do it, it is sin for them."

Proverbs 28:13 reminds us that "Whoever conceals their sins does not prosper, but the one who confesses and renounces them finds mercy."

If you hear of an instance where ineffective communication is stifling a relationship and you care, it is your responsibility to move the parties toward healthy communication as soon as possible. If you are the head of your household, you are responsible for facilitating the resolution of problems as they pertain to your family, since you are the leader.

If you have a meaningful relationship with either party, you are involved. Vigilance is required of everyone in order to keep our relationships healthy.

If there are obstacles to communicating one-on-one, ask a neutral person or two to sit in and mediate. If—and only *if*—we take this responsibility seriously will we then be able to eradicate this weakness in our community.

 I Hear You

TEST 2

(Answers in Appendix B)

1. Ineffective communication impacts relationships negatively by creating _____.

2. _____ make a poor engine because they will usually run the train right off the track.

3. Hurt people tend not to think clearly and therefore require an additional measure of _____.

4. Each individual is charged with the responsibility of confirming the _____ of _____ heard before reacting to them.

5. When communicating with someone who is hurt, the receiver is focused on listening for the _____ that is stated.

6. When communicating, it is important to remove all _____ from the setting.

7. The _____ is usually a poor listener who believes the contrary.

 I Hear You

8. The _____ usually thinks he or she is a _____ but is truly the aggressor.

9. The _____ will usually choose to absorb the unfair treatment of others despite feeling mistreated.

10. The _____ openly admits to disliking confrontation and will purposefully try to avoid it.

11. The _____ will seek conflict resolution quickly and effectively solves problems.

12. The message is the property of the _____.

 I Hear You

THE BIG BANG *(THE MOST NEGATIVE CYCLE OF HURT)*

One clearly identified cycle with a strong negative impact is what I call "The Big Bang". It is one of the most commonly seen reactions in relationships. It is observed when one party in an instance of communication becomes the recipient of speech or action that is perceived as offensive. The individual then responds quickly with heightened emotion, releasing negative speech or behavior that repels the sender. This instance is then followed by a

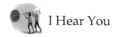

period of time during which there are instances of disrespectful, passively aggressive, or overtly aggressive verbal exchanges or behaviors. It can occur as simply as it does in the upcoming case study.

CASE STUDY (THE TOILET PAPER INCIDENT)

Meet Steve and Paula, a couple married for six months. One evening Paula went into their bathroom and later emerged enraged. She approached Steve angrily. "I am sick and tired of you putting the toilet paper on the holder so it rolls off from underneath instead of over! Every time I go into the bathroom after you change it, it is unreeling from underneath and you know I like it the other way." "Wait a minute. It doesn't even matter to me which way it comes off," he replied in defense. "That is because you don't care what I like. You should have known better. You only think about yourself!" She stated as she walked away angrily. Steve was hurt. He had taken notice that she always put the toilet paper on the reel flowing over instead of under, but did not apply any significance to it. He felt disrespected and trampled upon. Paula did not speak to Steve for the rest of that evening. The next morning, Paula left home

without kissing him as she usually did. "We have only been married six months and he is already losing interest. He never does anything the way I want it." She thought to herself. She was also hurt. Steve called her several times during the day, but she refused to discuss the matter with him. All day she pondered over how he could be so inconsiderate.

(See commentary in Appendix C.)

QUESTIONS (Write your answers on a separate sheet of paper.)

1. What do you see in their interaction that is negative or ineffective?

2. What could have been done to prevent this charged interaction?

3. What is happening to their relationship and why?

4. What thoughts do you have regarding Paula's statement that Steve should have known better?

5. What self-fulfilling prophesy is Paula engaging in? What self-injury did she cause?

The driver of these types of interactions may believe that he or she is protecting self, but the reality is, this hurtful individual is consciously choosing behavior and speech that injures the recipient and undermines the relationship. As the fog begins to clear, this person may become plagued with remorse and/or guilt, yielding personal injury as another product of this negative cycle. The irony here is that the actions of the receiver, which may have originally been intended to protect self, cause hurt to all parties involved.

1. Why did Paula verbally attack Steve?
2. What may she have been trying to protect about herself?
3. What will happen to the relationship over time if these sudden attacks are not brought under control?

This learned, detrimental pattern of behavior is profoundly negative. Consciously or not, the longer this cycle plagues the relationship, the more the aggressor begins to justify his or her actions. This justification ultimately issues a form of self-licensure to disregard and inflict hurt upon another. Recipients struggling with this emotional roller coaster will endure painful attacks and neglect, as the driver of this cycle formulates unfounded myths resulting from faulty reasoning and then takes negative action in self-defense.

Hearts may begin to harden. The injured person may begin to withdraw in many ways. The withdrawal tends to isolate both parties in this cycle. Unable to reach resolution due to unhealthy communication, some individuals—perpetrator as well as receiver—may begin to turn to others outside the relationship for comfort. This action becomes the catalyst for emotional starvation, causing the relationship to become emotionally emaciated. Some individuals, due to multiple failed attempts at getting the attacker to see the injury caused by this action, will tolerate the abuse until it becomes unbearably terminal and kills the relationship. This single cycle, if allowed to go unbroken, has the potential to send the relationship into cardiac arrest. If you identify this cycle in your relationship, take action now. Break it before your relationship becomes food for the cancer that consumes relationships.

When you sense that your feelings have been stirred, or when something or someone offends you, overcome the urge to verbally attack the source of the disruption to your emotional balance and simply ask questions to see if there is validity to your feelings of indignation. When someone makes a statement or performs an action that stirs

your emotions, you should quickly inform the offender of what happened and how it made you feel. This statement should be followed by a pause, which allows the offender time to respond. Avoid adding anything to the statement until the receiver gives feedback that addresses the statement of hurt. Most people will choose particular actions for reasons known and understood only by them. Actions are not always intended to offend. Another appropriate response is to go to that person and ask clarifying questions that can initiate discussion and subsequent clarification of the matter at hand.

The key to preventing and breaking this cycle is the voluntary verbal exposure of the hurt and the vigilance and skill of the receiver in identifying and addressing the feeling expressed. If a feeling is not exposed, it cannot be addressed. The personal repetitive visitation of hurt feelings can skew perception and harden even the kindest of hearts.

Unless someone commits an offense that violates a clearly established rule governing the relationship, responding to someone with the statement "You should have known better" when someone makes a mistake is a reflection of one's emotional laziness.

Separate human beings are just that. They are separate. They have individual thoughts that lead to different perceptions. Differing responses to the same set of stimuli require the exchange of thoughts and feelings to enhance and integrate the understanding of the parties involved. Telling someone that they should know one's position or interpretation implies that the individual is expected to do so without one expending the effort required to share it. The owner of this position or statement is expressing him or herself from a position of complacency with no regard for the receiver's individuality.

"The words of the reckless pierce like swords, but the tongue of the wise brings healing." **(Prov. 12:18)**

Failing to clarify one's perception of an action or message before responding negatively is a pitfall that yields profoundly complex, deeply seated, negative emotions. These emotions skew perception and place stress on the relationship.

QUESTIONS

1. Are you mired in the pattern of reacting sensitively to the words and actions of others without seeking clarification?

2. If so, did something happen singularly or repeatedly in your upbringing to cause you to feel the need to protect yourself from hurt?

3. During your formative years, were you given the opportunity or encouraged to express your feelings?

If you identify that you have difficulty expressing your feelings calmly and respectfully, are you willing to take action to ease that burden? One safe place for you to initiate the change is right here, right now. It starts with ownership.

 I Hear You

GOD'S GIFT TO MAN *(THE ABILITY TO SOOTHE HURT)*

It is my belief that God gave parents the instinctive ability to address hurt, thereby removing it. This can be observed in the interactions between a parent and child. In most cases, the instant a parent detects hurt in a child, he or she will institute measures to soothe or remove it. However, when an individual is exposed to repeated hurt, the abuse has the potential to repress this ability. When

 I Hear You

this willingness to address the hurt of others is repressed, it can lead to a perpetual cycle of hurt people causing hurt to others. Emotion has neither age nor gender. It is neither right nor wrong. It simply is what it is.

We must always remember that the actions we take when we become the host to emotions can define us in the eyes of others.

CASE STUDY (SELECTIVE SOOTHING)

A two-year-old male is playing with a cabinet door. He repeatedly opens and closes it with amusement. On one attempt to close it, he is too slow at removing his hand from the door's edge and he accidentally slams his fingers. Distressed and seeking comfort, he runs to his mother (Cindy), tearfully reaching upward with the injured hand. Realizing what has transpired, she picks him up and hugs him, then she kisses his fingers. Afterward she puts him down. Feeling comforted, he runs back to the door and resumes the same set of actions that led to his previous injury. Her husband Carlos looks on with admiration and smiles.

Later that evening, when approached by her husband of ten years to discuss the hurt she caused

him by calling him a pig the night before, Cindy becomes indignant and begins yelling at him, stating, "You shouldn't have left your dirty dishes in the sink! I had just emptied it." She then walks into their bedroom and closes the door. She had discussed this issue with him previously. She had made it quite clear that after she washes the dishes, she expects the sink to remain cleared for the rest of the night. Feeling mistreated, Carlos clenches his fists and walks away.

(See commentary in Appendix C.)

QUESTIONS

1. What are your thoughts regarding this interaction?
2. What message is Cindy sending her husband?
3. What other action could Cindy have taken?
4. Do you see this element (failing to address stated feelings) in your present communication style? What can you do to help yourself begin to focus on stated feelings?

When someone approaches us with a feeling, the feeling is neither wrong nor right. He or she is simply the host to an emotion with a need. If we personalize the expression of the feeling and react with indignation and blame, we are sending the message that we are not safe to approach and we will display a lack of concern for the expressed emotion. That person will be less likely to seek your attention when the next occasion arrives in which there is a need for emotional comfort. In an intimate relationship where there is routinely reciprocal giving, this inability to address emotion without personalizing the issue has the potential to cause one to not only be viewed as unapproachable, but as ungrateful, as well.

Each emotion has a need that is irrespective of age and gender. Fear, anger, and anxiety need to be calmed.

Hurt needs to be soothed. A 250-pound 50-year-old male has the same need for emotional soothing as a dependent two-year-old. We must purpose to become vigilant in our effort to identify and repair the damage caused by words and actions. This renewed vigilance will equip us to win the fight against the cancer that so readily consumes relationships. This vigilance will help us to remain tender-hearted and loving in the eyes of those who need us. We will be viewed as a safe haven for the expression of emotional needs as they arise.

Listen for the words expressing the hurt, then tenderly address the feeling. Happiness is allowing feelings to be what they are instead of what we think they should be.

CHALLENGE

The next time someone comes to you and states what they are feeling, evaluate whether or not you immediately addressed the feeling stated, or if your response ignored the feeling that you heard.

 I Hear You

NOTHING MORE THAN FEELINGS
(Hearing Spoken Feelings)

Once the feeling is addressed, most individuals will pay less attention to what happened subsequent to the initial offense. The offended party must effectively state the feelings that were raised as a result of an issue by using feeling words. It is important to have the feelings surrounding an issue addressed quickly. It is not important to try to force someone to agree with your position; the motivation for actions and behavior are sometimes

 I Hear You

only understood by their source. The sender's position doesn't automatically mean he or she intentionally tried to harm you. It is beneficial for the hurt party to state to the sender of a message how an action or statement caused him or her to feel without accusing the sender of anything or calling him or her names. Name-calling is hurtful.

Be aware that after addressing the feelings of an individual, the intent of the message will usually be explained instinctively. The hurt party must be willing to **listen** in order to identify how the intention differs from his or her perception. The person who delivered the hurt should do more than listen to the spoken feelings; he or she should offer an apology to the recipient of the hurt and be willing to discuss ways in which that type of hurt can be avoided in the future. Taking responsibility for hurtful speech or actions expresses that you care about the other person's emotional wellbeing.

KEY POINT

When communicating with someone who is visibly upset, the goal is to get to the heart of what that person is feeling as quickly as possible and extinguish the emotional fire by addressing the

 I Hear You

feeling. Once this is accomplished, normal, healthy communication will usually resume.

QUESTIONS:

1. If someone offends you (purposefully or not), what should your first action be?
2. What are some of the things that prevent us from sharing our feelings with others?

Matthew 18:15 reminds us, "If your brother or sister sins, go and point out their fault, just between the two of you. If they listen to you, you have won them over."

When do we go to them?

According to **Matthew 5:23**, "Therefore, if you are offering your gift at the altar and there remember that your brother or sister has something against you, leave your gift there in front of the altar. First go and be reconciled to them; then come and offer your gift."

REMINDER:

Hurt people will sometimes attack in defense or step away. One must avoid attacking the sender of the message because one initially feels hurt after receiving it. The first and most important actions should be to clarify the message received, state

what happened, and how it caused you to feel. Stepping away is often an effort at self-control or protection from repeated hurt. It also sacrifices the relationship if the move is final. After repeated attacks, an individual will often step away to avoid attacking in defense.

 I Hear You

ATTACK VS. OPINION

Read each sentence below. If you believe it is an attack, circle the "A". If you believe it is an opinion, circle the "O". (See answers in Appendix A.)

1. "I just didn't see that as the best decision." A O
2. "You are inconsiderate." A O
3. "From my perspective I don't see where I was being considered by that action." A O
4. "When I was sick and didn't hear from you, I didn't think you cared." A O
5. "You are heartless and don't care anything about my wellbeing." A O
6. "You just think you are better than I am." A O
7. "You are an idiot." A O
8. "I just feel like you are always thinking about yourself." A O
9. "You are a hypocrite." A O
10. "You are a screw-up." A O

These important focal points address how to communicate with an offender:

- Do it without anger or blame.

- Express how things made you feel.
- Avoid placing the focus on who is right and who is wrong.

KEY POINT

Unless there are obvious barriers, failing to honor a request for direct communication sends the message that you are not interested in the relationship. If that is your position, then you should display courage by saying it directly so there will be no further expectations. Doing so is more respectful than avoiding the situation.

 I Hear You

SENSITIVE OR INSENSITIVE?

Please answer the following questions based on whether your significant other exhibits these actions or not. After completing the questionnaire, please exchange your sheet for that of your significant other. Divide the total number of "Yes" answers by the number of questions on the page. The percentage is a reflection of the degree of sensitivity you currently exhibit through the eyes of your significant other, based on these questions.

Does your significant other:

1. Give hugs and kisses when you need comfort? YES NO

2. Choose words carefully in an effort to avoid hurting your feelings? YES NO

3. Encourage the expression of your feelings when you have concerns? YES NO

4. Willingly perform tasks to help lighten your load when possible? YES NO

5. Respond quickly when you directly state that you need something? YES NO

6. Avoid being verbally abusive toward you when he/she is angry? YES NO

 I Hear You

7. Demonstrate a desire to spend time with you?
   YES   NO

8. Compliment you on your appearance?
   YES   NO

9. Avoid randomly saying things that are unkind?
   YES   NO

10. Avoid doing things that are deliberately spiteful?   YES   NO

11. Demonstrate an interest in your opinion?
    YES   NO

12. Think about you when he or she is not at home?
    YES   NO

13. Give acts of affection just because?
    YES   NO

SCORE = _____

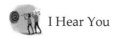

EMOTIONAL BURDEN VS. EMOTIONAL STARVATION
(Insensitivity)

As mentioned in the section called "God's Gift to Man", I believe the skill of addressing emotion is something that is naturally passed on from parent to child via active demonstration. When we are reared by parents who are inept in this area of development, there is a strong likelihood that we will also be inept when it comes to displaying and receiving emotional sensitivity.

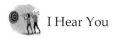

Without intervention, insensitive people may not become aware of their insensitivity. When challenged to give of themselves in this area, they may feel frustration due to the level of difficulty. Children of insensitive parents quickly learn to store away their feelings due to the resistance that is met when they attempt to have their emotional needs addressed. Years of having feelings go unaddressed can result in the feelings being stored away and compressed. They become scabbed-over for protection. This scab becomes increasingly thinner over time. Eventually the scab will be brushed by something perceived as abrasive. Whether intentional or not, the brushing of this scab will result in a violent outpouring of feelings. Let's take a look at an interesting couple.

CASE STUDY (WHERE IS THE LOVE?)

Thirty-year-old Cory grew up in a household with both parents and two siblings. One sibling is two years older. The other is two years younger. By the time he reached age 22, he had two children and was bouncing from one entry level job to another. He felt unfulfilled and frustrated. While living with his parents, Cory was subject to verbal attacks that came without warning. He was often attacked for things he had neither done nor had involvement with. When he tried to explain, his words often went unheard and he was often seen as a back talker. These sudden verbal attacks would often lead to physical attacks, as well. He learned to keep his opinions to himself and go with the flow. He simply wanted to keep the peace. The insults were less severe when he did that.

At age 19, Cory couldn't take it anymore, so he moved out of his parents' home and started life on his own. He always wanted to have a successful career and a loving family of his own. After moving away from home, he took a job working in a local store. That is where he met Elizabeth. She was drawn to him immediately because she admired his quiet nature. They quickly fell in love and moved in together to ease their financial burden. They both wanted to be married, but thought it would be better to wait until they could afford it. Not long after they moved in together, Elizabeth became pregnant with their first child. They were ecstatic. Eighteen months later, they had their second child. Cory picked up a second job while Elizabeth stayed home with the children. Child care was entirely too expensive, so it was best for her not to work. The happy couple soon found themselves dealing with the day-to-day stressors of life.

Elizabeth became frustrated with Cory because he never wanted to talk. She pleaded with him to be open with her. When she asked him to tell her how he was feeling, he would make excuses not to. If she was able to corner him, he would explode before she was able to completely get her thought out, then he would walk away. He didn't understand why she wanted to talk about everything. Talking always led to more problems. She always wanted to know how he felt, but all she would get was, "I don't know." Elizabeth felt isolated and disconnected. Cory felt cornered and was more at peace when he was away at work.

(See commentary in Appendix C.)

QUESTIONS:

1. What do you see happening in this family?
2. What evidence is there of a slow death occurring in their relationship?
3. Which actions could they take to begin steering their relationship in the right direction?

Years of compressing feelings not only inhibit a person's ability to identify and express his own feelings, it greatly inhibits the person's ability to address the feelings of others. This is due to inhibition and lack of practice. If this practice develops during childhood, in later years as the child becomes an adult and enters into intimate relationships, he can display dysfunction in this area. He may develop feelings of inadequacy as his relationship begins to challenge him to give emotional support and address the emotional needs of his partner. He may unfairly expect his partner to know what he is feeling without him having to state it. He may also demonstrate anger towards his partner when his confused partner asks him to put his feelings into words instead of negative behaviors. It is an unreasonable expectation to think that someone can know what you are feeling without you properly stating it. It is equally unreasonable to think that you can thoroughly understand what someone is feeling or thinking without it being stated. One's display of anger does not state what one is feeling. Displays of anger are nothing less than threatening behaviors. Relationships such as this will struggle with varying degrees of emotional disconnect.

 I Hear You

When involved in an intimate relationship with someone who is oppressively dominant and refuses to engage in conversation that facilitates expression of feelings and ideas, the same type of painful confusion may be experienced due to the conscious or subconscious insensitivity. One of the greatest needs of humans is the need to be heard. This type of oppression is not only disrespectful, it is painful. When the pain becomes great enough, individuals who choose not to speak or are not given the opportunity to do so, may begin to repress their feelings and thoughts. These emotions will remain stored, thus waiting to be uncovered. When the covering is removed—triggered by visual or auditory stimuli—there may be an eruption of feeling which is usually disproportionate to the immediate situation. The host of these eruptions is often confused or embarrassed by his sudden shift in mood and the intensity of the release.

It is possible for the person who enters this relationship healthy to begin to withdraw after repeatedly being hurt by the unhealthy partner. The pain may become too great due to the undeveloped skill of addressing each other's emotions and the lack of knowledge regarding how to develop an ability in this area. Some individuals in this situation may find it easy to blame their inability on the opposing party in the relationship and may seek to escape by starting another relationship that is more superficial and does not challenge him or her in this area. The lack of depth and shallow emotional commitment may ease the stress of intimately relating, thereby giving a false sense of happiness, which can ultimately lead to the formation of one or more relationships outside of the one to which this individual is bound. As time elapses and these outside relationships become more serious, this person may develop an unhealthy pattern of hopping from one relationship to another in his or her quest for the "happy feeling". The quest for this emotional high is a form of self-medicating and can become so addictive that some will violate their moral beliefs in search of it. Some may also transition to substance abuse during their quest for relief of the emotional pain. The difficulty in identifying the source of the pain is evident in the fact that some will remain in denial after the source is shown to them. The true source may be difficult for this individual to identify due to presuppositions that have been deeply inscribed and personally identified as the source of the pain. The person involved in a relationship with this individual can potentially fall victim to the cycle of a hurt person hurting another. The relationship may end up weakened and eventually devoured by the cancer that consumes relationships. When presented with these challenges, we must be careful not to cast blame, but simply seek to identify and then develop the weaker partner before the relationship is devoured.

It is worth noting that the individual who gravitates to anger routinely and has great difficulty expressing tender emotions is likely to be in deep emotional pain. In order to help this individual, one has to look beyond the anger and see the pain. It is ironic that these individuals who are in great need of soothing and tenderness tend to reject it when it is offered. They tend to pull away from the loving touch since they are not accustomed to it or feel they do not deserve it. This pulling away can cause others to feel rejected, which causes others to withdraw from them. This withdrawal can be seen as confirmation of the message received in their childhood: the message that they are not worthy of love, or the myth that their significant other does not truly love them. When our loved one offers us loving soothing touch, we should pause and absorb it. This is part of God's gift to man.

Individuals in pain will sometimes give themselves permission to be physically and emotionally hurtful to others. It is important that people in this person's immediate circle express the pain that is experienced by this person's actions and thereby bring into focus the product of the hurtful actions or words. If sugar is to effectively sweeten water, it must be stirred. This stirring of the attacker's awareness will sometimes bring about remorse and empathy, which are helpful catalysts to behavioral change. Couples or families who discover this component as part of their dynamic must be dutiful in their effort to identify the angry, unloving behaviors and replace them with gentle, loving ones. After purging the unloving, detrimental behaviors, logically speaking, what will remain are the loving, sustaining behaviors. Loving behaviors will nourish the relationships back to health. We must strive to overcome the fear of rejection and the discomfort associated with performing loving actions. These behaviors are innate but can become suppressed with prolonged exposure to physical and psychological abuse. The fear and discomfort should be viewed as nothing less than restrictive emotions. These emotions, if allowed to go unchecked, will fortify the negative cycles seen in association with ineffective communication. They have the potential to divide and conquer individuals of the family unit, thereby eroding its support. We must be willing to push these emotions aside for the loving sustenance that waits ahead.

The person who lacks sensitivity may attempt to compensate in various ways. Some individuals compensate by trying to express their feelings

 I Hear You

through actions performed, such as kind tasks and gift-giving. While these things are nice to do, they are ineffective when it comes to emptying the storage bin of feelings.

While one partner may feel burdened by the need to address emotions, the other may feel like he or she is starving for emotional sustenance.

Human beings have basic emotional needs. One such need is to have feelings addressed when the need arises. When people of differing backgrounds come together in a union, having the ability to respond in a sensitive manner to expressed emotions will feed that union and aid it to flourish. On the contrary, the absence of this ability is a recipe for conflict. Chronic insensitivity is a pitfall that is capable of producing an aftermath of deep emotional pain.

KEY POINT

It can be very difficult to identify and address someone who does not have the same level of competency when it comes to expressing their feelings. The healthy partner in this interpersonal relationship will need to exercise patience and longsuffering in order to persevere and eventually overcome many complex issues. If we find

ourselves struggling to listen attentively so we can address the emotional need of our significant other, it could be because we were never trained through active demonstration to do so. We must be diligent in examining ourselves in order to discover if we need development in this basic area of communication.

QUESTIONS

1. Are you able to respond in a sensitive manner to someone who has come to you with a concern or with hurt feelings?

2. Does your temper flare when someone approaches you to discuss feelings they possess based on some action for which you are responsible?

3. If so, why do you think you respond in this manner?

 I Hear You

THE STRUGGLING MIND *(THE PRODUCT OF MISTRUST)*

In order to optimize our emotional development, we must be willing to trust the authority figures around us during our formative years. They are our primary source of knowledge and training. When exposed to individuals who are insensitive, abusive, or simply unaware of how to support healthy emotional growth, we learn very quickly to protect ourselves by limiting our exposure to the pain that accompanies the insensitivity. If there is a

frequent need to protect ourselves emotionally, it is likely that we will begin to form deep-seated mistrust, which can become a normal way of life. If not removed, mistrust will likely stunt our emotional development. The lack of trust will restrict our desire to seek information from outside sources, which will in turn hinder our emotional growth.

Conflict can arise as we find ourselves physically developed but emotionally immature. Those around us may expect us to be better emotionally equipped. Failure to meet those expectations may lead to feelings of inadequacy due to the mismatch of physical and emotional development.

The inability to trust, which began in our youth, can transfer to our adulthood and place stress on our personal relationships. The adult full of mistrust may have a desire for a close connection with others, but the mistrust gives rise to accusations and misperceptions that sabotage those relationships before they can properly mature. It can ultimately color the perception of what is seen and heard. Firmly-seated mistrust causes a host of problems that can lead to issues of poor self-esteem and self-image due to stunted emotional growth.

Trust is a necessary building block for a stable relationship. Our emotional lives are less complicated with this block firmly seated in its place.

When making the statement, "I don't trust you, this, or that, because ...," the word *because* should appropriately be followed by an admission of what we are afraid of. Example: "I don't trust being in a relationship with you because I am afraid of being hurt."

We are commanded by scripture to love one another. **John 13:34-35** states, "A new command I give you: Love one another. As I have loved you, so you must love one another. By this everyone will know that you are my disciples, if you love one another." If you are to demonstrate love that is perfect, you must push through, overcome the fear, and trust each other. Mistrust is yet another pitfall. It is capable of yielding pain and confusion.

 I Hear You

CASE STUDY (THE AFTERMATH OF HURT)

Cheryl is a 34-year-old female who is married with two children. Cheryl grew up in a home as the youngest of four children. She was always a sensitive child. Her parents worked hard to provide for the family and were away from home often. Being the baby, as well as the only girl, her parents spoiled her. They were overprotective and restrictive. She also came from a home in which there was no structure to the communication. Her parents as well as siblings often aggressively accused each other of things that were unfounded. They would draw premature conclusions then quickly attack and cast blame. Cheryl was a defiant teenager who became pregnant in her early teens. The father of her child was physically and emotionally abusive. He abandoned her and the gestating child. Filled with hurt, she later experimented with the use of drugs and alcohol in an attempt to numb the pain. Late in her pregnancy, she met a young man (Danny), who befriended her. He later married her and became a father to her son.

Subconsciously, Cheryl became a people-pleaser. She would eagerly perform tasks for others to gain their friendship and approval. Criticism angered her and would lead to her performing spiteful acts or launching unfounded verbal attacks.

As she settled into marriage, she tried eagerly to please her husband. She was flighty and would fall short of achieving mutual goals they set. She would forget to follow up on things from time to time. Despite the fact that she was full of emotion, Cheryl was emotionally closed and had difficulty expressing her feelings respectfully. Her most easily expressed emotion was anger. Whenever confronted, Cheryl would become anxious, angry, and defensive. The mere contemplation of a serious discussion would set her off and block her ability to have healthy conversations. There existed an obvious struggle to identify and express what she was feeling in clear terms. She was perplexing to her husband, who repeatedly felt disrespected due to her sudden explosions and nonverbal language. It was evident that she cared for him; she just did not know how to communicate with him.

(See commentary in Appendix C.)

 I Hear You

QUESTIONS

1. Can you identify the sources and products of mistrust in Cheryl's life?
2. Why did she become a people-pleaser?
3. What was it about criticism that aroused her anger?
4. Why did she become anxious when confronted?
5. What do you think made her so closed?
6. What do you see as the biggest obstacle to her communication?

Her husband Danny also came out of an abusive household. He was physically and emotionally abused by his mother. There were unpredictable times when she would withhold communication and then suddenly strike him in anger. This behavior led to much confusion and insecurity. He was distant. Outward displays of affection were foreign to him, but he soon learned that it met a need for him. As an adult, he was a perfectionist. He sought to have things done on schedule and always needed an answer when things were not done within his timeframe. He felt secure with things being done his way. He had the tendency to hold firmly to what he believed when challenged to receive and implement new information regarding his behaviors or his formulated ideas. He would demonstrate angry outbursts and demanded support from his wife when he became stressed. He reminded her constantly that the help she offered was not enough. Her desperate reply would be, "Please tell me what I did." He constantly came home from work and expressed his displeasure with this or that. "What have you been doing all day?" he would ask. He seemed to blame her for most things that went wrong. He began self-medicating with alcohol and eventually became an alcoholic. He was blind to the burden that alcoholism was placing on his family. He was angry and accused Cheryl of not loving or caring about him. He would leave home and not account for his whereabouts. He later became entangled in an illicit affair and blamed her for that also. His outward cry for love was very clear, yet the obstacles he presented to receiving it were unclear to him.

(See commentary in Appendix C.)

QUESTIONS

1. Can you identify the sources and products of mistrust in Cheryl and Danny's relationship?

2. What do you see as the biggest obstacle to this couple's communication?

3. What is the significance of Danny's substance abuse?

4. Why do you think Danny was so critical of his wife?

CHALLENGE

Do you find yourself demonstrating an underlying, unfounded mistrust in your close relationships? If so, take some time to try and identify where it originated, then try to implement measures to eliminate it. Try to override your feelings of mistrust by first exposing them to the person or people with whom you have a close, meaningful relationship.

REMOVING THE CORK (*REVEALING ONE'S HURT*)

Exposing our hurt is not a sign of weakness. Contrary to popular belief, it takes great strength and confidence to reveal our pain. If we are to gain loving emotional sustenance, we simply must be willing to tell our loved ones when we are hurt and the identified source of the pain. Feeling hurt does not give us the right to, in turn, hurt someone with harsh words or actions. In fact, if we are willing to trust the source of our perceived hurt and reveal it

 I Hear You

to him or her, we may find that the words or actions causing the hurt originated with a different intention. Some individuals forfeit a lifetime of blissful intimacy because they succumb to the notion that they have to be tough. This person spends a lifetime building a wall that becomes so high and so firmly erected that no one can overcome it and offer them loving emotional sustenance.

When we fail to disclose our feelings to each other, we tend to store up negative emotions that feed misperceptions. When these emotions become burdensome and can no longer be contained, they will ultimately erupt in the form of negative speech and behavior.

 I Hear You

These actions are in turn hurtful to the recipient. We simply must develop the skill of releasing emotions by clearly stating our feelings. It is imperative that we also master the art of asking a clarifying question to be sure our perception is accurate. This action is vital to maintaining emotional wellbeing and decreasing the stress placed on our relationships. Failing to do so is a flagrant injustice to oneself. We were created as neuropsychological beings and therefore are at risk for emotional harm if we allow ourselves to remain in a prolonged heightened emotional state. This sustained practice has the potential of heightening mistrust and hardening our heart. Mistrust hinders our willingness to assimilate new information and stunts our emotional growth.

QUESTIONS

1. Are you able to listen selflessly as your loved one explains what he or she is feeling?
2. Do you listen with the intent of identifying where support is needed?
3. Have you begun taking steps toward expressing your feelings more clearly if needed?

 I Hear You

CHALLENGE

Take some personal time to examine whether or not you are storing your feelings or expressing them in a healthy manner.

 I Hear You

COMPOUNDING THE HURT
(SPITEFULNESS)

Spitefulness is composed of cruel, vengeful acts done to inflict harm on another person. These acts are usually done in response to actual or perceived hurt. Perceived hurt is real to the person who perceives it. Spitefulness is not Christ-like behavior, and according to **James 4:17** it is sin to the person who commits it. The verse says, "If anyone, then knows the good they ought to do and doesn't do it, it is sin for them." Acts of spitefulness or inconsideration do nothing more than compound hurt, which drives daggers into the heart of the relationship.

Spitefulness is learned behavior that hinders healthy communication. It is both premeditated and hurtful. As stated earlier, one purpose of communication is to remove unintentional and intentional hurt. Spiteful acts are selfish and convey the message that whenever events do not proceed as I expect them to, I will hurt you. We should be diligent about evaluating the motivation behind the actions we take.

These purposeful, negative actions have no place in a loving relationship.

If one finds himself performing a restrictive, hurtful action against another that is motivated by actual or perceived hurt, one should evaluate the action to see if it is, in fact, sinful in nature. Scripture guides us to be tender with one another. **Ephesians 5:33** states, "However, each one of you also must love his wife as he loves himself, and the wife must respect her husband."

Spitefulness is a major contributor to the cycle of hurt people hurting people. Spitefulness is evil and is surely a pitfall. We must exercise caution not to get involved in these types of behaviors in fear that they will consume us. The progression is very subtle. The person who derives satisfaction from willingly delivering hurt to another person, whether aware or not, is classified as an abuser. **Matthew 12:37** states, "For by your words you will be acquitted, and by your words you will be condemned." The words and actions we speak or perform against another are capable of bringing us spiritual condemnation.

The recipient of these actions will quickly learn not to trust the sender of these messages. He or she will begin to feel unsafe when this attacker is displeased. In order to escape Satan's grasp, the attacker involved in spiteful acts must be willing to examine himself in order to discover the negative emotion that is driving the spitefulness. The proper action for this attacker to take in addressing these emotions is simply to go to the recipient of the spiteful act and state what happened, as well as the resulting emotions generated by the event. This action will give the receiver an opportunity to address the feelings of hurt. This attacker must be willing to take responsibility for hurtful actions by issuing an apology.

 I Hear You

An apology pours cool water on the blazing fire of hurt.

CHALLENGE

Take some personal time and evaluate whether or not you actively engage in spiteful behaviors. If so, what actions can you employ in order to eliminate these behaviors?

 I Hear You

THE DEVIL'S MESSAGE
(BRAINWASHING OURSELVES)

The statements below represent some of the messages we tend to tell ourselves when we engage in negative self-talk. This type of one-sided conversation is powerful. It has the ability to skew our perceptions and alter our view of our loved ones. If you find yourself engaging in this type of talk, quickly dismissing it may be the best course of action.

I Hear You

1. My spouse/significant other does not respect me. (Sometimes actions and words seem disrespectful. Target the behavior, not the person.)
2. My spouse/significant other does not wish me well. (Is your loved one really ill-willed?)
3. My spouse/significant other sees me as lesser. (Do you see yourself as lesser?)
4. My spouse/significant other does not love me. (Unless one is told this, one should simply target the behaviors that seem unloving.)
5. My spouse/significant other is using me for self-gain. (Is your spouse really ill-willed?)
6. I'm a bad person. Bad people need to be punished. (How do others see you?)
7. No one will ever love me because I am unlovable. (Ask your loved one if he or she loves you.)
8. I never have been very smart. (Ask your loved one if you are smart.)

START: Telling yourself the opposite of these things and reverse the messages.

STOP: Viewing your world through filters. Stop projecting your views onto others. Use the communication model. Clarify the message.

Brainwashing yourself with false notions is a pitfall, and a hindrance to communication. The person who lacks the trust required to ask questions regarding thoughts he has already processed, runs the risk of inscribing these false notions until they become reassuringly familiar. At that point, confirmation of those thoughts may seem evident even if they do not exist. The feelings brought on by the false confirmation makes a swift knee-jerk reaction more likely. The pitfall lies in the fact that these notions cause pain, which may give rise to a defensive, angry response to an inaccurate message. At that point the perception has become the reality. This angry response is unfair to the receiver who may attempt to offer the clarification needed in an effort to calm the emotion. The sad fact is that people with these deeply-seated myths tend not to hear well.

The recipient of these accusations must learn not to engage in the performance of actions that are aimed at disproving these myths. Doing so will never fill the void in the bottomless pit of insecurity

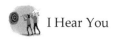

and low self-esteem. One simply needs to live above reproach and allow one's actions and life choices to do the speaking. An occasional gentle word of encouragement to let go of the myths may also be effective.

It is important to understand the value of asking questions directly in order to prevent the formulation and firm seating of myths. One ought to practice immediately asking clarifying questions regarding issues that cause one's emotions to stir. Some individuals have a great deal of reluctance to do just that. We should not offer ourselves excuses that prevent us from asking necessary questions. It is easy to unwittingly develop the pattern of processing events through a filter that supports a preconceived notion. These types of filters can color events in a manner that puts us at a disadvantage when it comes to identifying the facts surrounding it. Our misinterpretation of the events sometimes becomes the source of our own pain and the initiator of conflict.

CASE STUDY (HELP ME SEE CLEARLY)

Jarred is a 23-year-old male blessed with naturally good looks. At age 23, he met Tangie. They seemed to be a perfect match. They dated for four years and

 I Hear You

then were married. Tangie adored him. Not long after their union, Tangie noticed that Jarred exhibited a pattern of making accusations about things that simply were not true. Jarred routinely made the statement that he wasn't stupid and that she just needed to take responsibility for what she had done. When she tried to correct his misperceptions, he would root down in his position and become angry. He would further accuse her of trying to justify (what he saw to be) her wrong actions. This behavior continued for years. He later began to accuse her of not listening to him and not caring how he felt. He began engaging in punishing behaviors. He would go days without speaking to her. When the phone rang, he would pick it up and speak politely to the caller. When he ended the call, he would resume his cold, spiteful behaviors toward Tangie. Tangie noted that when there were issues with Jarred and his siblings, they would not come together and lovingly speak about the issues. They all made assumptions then approached each other in anger. She pleaded with him to listen to reason, but he refused. He accused her of all sorts of things. Feeling hurt, he began to confide in a female coworker who offered him a sympathetic ear.

 I Hear You

In a short period of time, they entered into an illicit sexual affair. Jarred would come home and start arguments so he could storm out and meet Charlene, whom he believed genuinely loved him because she listened to him. Charlene was married and knew that he was, also. Tangie did not know how to reach him because he would not hear her. She did not know why he gravitated to such a negative picture of her. When she became angry and frustrated, Jarred saw it as further confirmation that he was right about her. She was hurt and emotionally damaged. In desperation, she would ask him to sit down and talk with her. He refused to discuss the affair with her and said it was her fault because she was not giving him what he needed. She refused to be defined as the person he had in his mind. She no longer trusted him. She saw him as confused, angry, and abusive. Feeling hopeless, she called an attorney and informed Jarred that she was filing for divorce. The irony of the whole situation was that she deeply loved Jarred.

The couple later underwent counseling and discovered that Jarred had been the victim of emotional and sexual abuse as a teenager. They were able to overcome the communication and trust issues and salvaged their marriage.

(See commentary in Appendix C.)

During formative years, if an individual is reared in a household in which the parents are remiss when it comes to encouraging the expression of feelings and ideas, the child may develop the impression that his or her opinion is not valued. This belief may cause the child to become very reserved in the expression of feelings and opinions. In later years when that individual enters into a close personal relationship, this practice of reserving these expressions will already be well-seated and subconsciously put into practice. If the significant other freely expresses his or her feelings and opinions, the individual with the reservation may begin to cast blame for the deficiency by expressing thoughts such as "You don't care how I feel" or "You don't value my opinion because you never ask." Conflict may ensue as this myth begins to color even the simplest of interactions.

The person who formulates misperceptions based on their reluctance to ask questions will falsely accuse and thereby disrespect other individuals. This pattern is usually associated with low self-esteem and low self-image. The ideas formulated by these individuals will usually be revisited in their minds repeatedly over time before they are expressed, and therefore are usually solidified into belief and become a reality for the individual. When refuted, this individual will usually mount a strong defense of that position. Due to the lack of investigation, which is likely due to mistrust, this individual will usually accuse and may later be embarrassed to find that he or she is in a position of error. He or she may then try to find other reasons to adhere to the false notion, rather than admitting that their position was taken prematurely and in error.

People who willingly share ideas and feelings will wonder why this person struggles to express what comes naturally to them. When in conflict with this person, they may wonder what they may have done to cause this level of mistrust; why there is an obstacle that prevents their significant other from freely sharing with them. When constantly colored by a negative light, they may begin to fight against the bombardment of false images and notions. The fear may be that these notions will redefine them if allowed to go unchecked. This is a true recipe for conflict. The answer may rest in the simple fact that the host of these false ideas has difficulty in this area because he or she spent most of their life with a reservation regarding confrontation. He or she may also be defensive and mistrustful due to prior abuse, and is out of the practice of clarifying. The effort exerted to stop this cycle is worth spending. Push through the excuses and the reluctance. Ask the questions.

 I Hear You

HELP ME UNDERSTAND (*Clarify to Know*)

One of the most detrimental obstacles to effective communication is what happens when we misinterpret someone's message (verbal or nonverbal) and then act upon it negatively without seeking understanding or clarification first. We must circumvent this problem by making sure we seek clarification when something stirs our emotions. It is of utmost importance that we make sure that we know the intent of a message before responding to it negatively. It is important to understand that drawing conclusions based solely upon our perception makes the assumption that everything we perceive is accurate and therefore warrants no investigation. That action puts one in a selfish, arrogant position. The negativity is further compounded when the offended party takes the concerns to a third party and continues to misrepresent the original intended message due to lack of clarification. This action dishonors the sender of the original message. The feelings of victimization and subsequent indignation and anger that follow this type of decision will ultimately yield conflict.

Communication is not a one-way street; therefore people in close intimate relationships should choose to communicate effectively, all playing by the same rules. Parties with differing expectations regarding communication are destined for conflict. Each household should adopt a standard of communication in order to decrease conflict. The pitfall with one-sided expectations is not always obvious. Expectations placed upon someone without consent will frequently lead to disappointment. This disappointment is a form of self-inflicted hurt that is usually projected upon another individual. It is unfair to expect someone to

perform based upon expectations to which they have not agreed. This disappointment, when transformed to hurt, can also lead to anger.

An angry response will not gain audience to the words spoken. It will usually elicit a defensive response from the receiver because of the anxiety generated by the angry approach. The receiver, when stressed by the angry response, will give more attention to the negative, angry behavior and less to the spoken words. The goal of communication is to have the receiver hear the words expressed and accurately comprehend the intended message.

Be mindful of the impact of body language and tone of voice. People who gesture normally in conversation will also gesture when they are full of emotion. It is helpful for the receiver to look past the gesturing and address the feelings of the sender when they are stated. One who gestures must be more cognizant of his or her nonverbal messages. Should the receiver find active gesturing offensive, he or she should express to the sender that the gesturing is inhibiting the effectiveness of the delivery.

 I Hear You

KEY POINT

The sender of the message knows its intended meaning and is the only source for the offended party to go to in order to seek clarification. Failure to do this is also a form of disrespect. Avoid going to someone else for clarification before going to the sender of the message.

QUESTIONS

1. Do you take the time to evaluate your understanding of a message before you respond to it?

2. What is likely to happen when we fail to state what we are feeling as a result of spoken words or actions that we perceive as offensive, then react in a negative manner?

3. Can you explain one way in which we inflict hurt upon ourselves that is directly related to our expectations?

THE HARDENED HEART (*SOLIDIFYING PREMATURE CONCLUSIONS*)

Individuals who are not conscious of the communication cycle will sometimes refuse to abandon their position of error. Their mind becomes closed to input once they draw premature conclusions and repeatedly revisit them without seeking clarification. What is this called? Brainwashing. This is a usually a deeply-seated behavior. With this individual, there is a strong tendency to personalize information received due to chronically referencing the world from an egocentric viewpoint. This selfish position contributes to the skewing of information. Relying on one's perception without clarification can be a symptom of deeply-seated mistrust resulting from emotional and/or physical injury. This mistrust makes it difficult to assimilate information that overrides one's perception. This individual is often seen as overly sensitive and very defensive due to what may be years of self-protection. Some of the sensitivity displayed may also be the product of backlash from making accusations that frequently lead to someone inflicting physical or emotional pain.

Another expected byproduct of the actual or perceived hurt is spitefulness. This negative response may be resulting from the belief that all actions or speech processed as hurtful by this individual, are done intentionally by the sender of the words or actions. This self-protective individual may then begin to associate the sender with pain. This association may then lead to the development of negative emotions directed toward the sender, which in turn may yield spiteful acts. When in a relationship, one should periodically evaluate his or her commitment to it. If one finds that he or she is willing to perform hurtful actions rather than react in a loving manner, it may be an indication that one's heart is hardened. One may need to evaluate whether or not he or she is consumed by painful thoughts. If so, it is time to address them. It is not uncommon for the sender to grow weary and lose patience with this individual after repeated efforts to clarify the message from which the misperception was generated. The receiver of the hurtful speech and actions may ultimately grow weary and exit the relationship for self-protection. The source of these painful memories may be found in misperceptions that were not clarified, or a previous experience that was processed as hurt. The triggers releasing the pain are found in the present relationship.

As stated earlier, during episodes of communication the sender owns the message and thereby owns the right to clarify it. One should not dominate conversation with one's perception of the message. Failing to clarify a message before solidifying one's perception of it is a pitfall. We should avoid making accusations based solely on our perception. One should always seek to understand the message by requesting then listening to the clarification of its intent before overreacting to it. One whose heart is hardened and has difficulty assimilating new information that differs from the formulated misperception is destined for conflict. It is possible for this individual to remain stuck, fearful, and defensive, clinging to what is familiar, despite its dysfunctional nature, for a long period of time.

The failure of the receiver to seek information before responding in anger causes communication breakdown. Both the sender and the receiver can end the interaction in frustration. It is important to recognize when the conversation begins to spin out of control and take proper action by tabling discussions for a later date and time.

CASE STUDY (I WANT IT MY WAY)

Nathaniel is a 42-year-old male. He is married for the second time and has two children. His aunt Patricia was once a very influential figure in his life. He would call on her for advice on everything from business to personal relationships. She and her husband spent countless hours counseling and advising him. He described her as the mother he never had. After approximately six years of marriage, Patricia came to realize that Nathaniel had a pattern of seeking advice only to manipulate it to meet his needs. When his failure to heed advice led to complications he would twist the details of the events in an effort to avoid taking responsibility. Nathaniel surrounded himself with those whom he identified as givers but seldom gave of himself for the benefit of others. He was always on the take. Patricia received many reports that Nathaniel was verbally abusive when he did not get his way, but found it hard to believe because he presented her with another image. Over time, Patricia also noticed that when she counseled Nathaniel and his wife, they frequently wound up on polar opposite sides when it came to details regarding an event. This likely meant that someone was not being truthful.

Of noted frequency, when Nathaniel lodged a complaint about a person to Patricia, she would encourage him to go to that person and express what he was feeling. He frequently did not follow through. During Nathaniel's divorce from his first wife, he engaged in an angry battle with his spouse and asked Patricia to do something that would draw her into the middle of their feud. If performed, this action would also cause her to violate her conscience. She refused and asked them both not to confide in her the details of their divorce. Patricia did not want to offer advice or perform an act that would be hurtful to either party.

Nathaniel was upset with his aunt and felt that she had abandoned him during a stressful time when he needed her. He called her disloyal, inconsistent, and hypocritical and began distancing himself from her. When she would call on him for the routine conversation they had once enjoyed, he spitefully sent her to voicemail then returned the call several days later saying, "I noticed a missed call." When Patricia noticed the position taken by her nephew, she tried to educate him regarding her decision by giving the information Nathaniel should have asked for but did not. However, it was too late. Nathaniel had hardened his heart. He occasionally emerged from behind his wall of defense only to launch verbal attacks that gave no indication what he was feeling. Many months went by and Nathaniel never made one request for a face-to-face conversation with his aunt. When Patricia grew weary of the name-calling and verbal attacks, she requested that the two families sit down for a face-to-face. When there was no reply, she severed all ties and stepped away to eliminate the stressors and the pain.

 I Hear You

(See commentary in Appendix C)

QUESTIONS

1. What action should have been taken early in this scenario that may have preserved the relationship?

2. Does it appear that the relationship was of equal value to both parties?

3. What are the indicators of a hardened heart?

4. Whose heart was hardened?

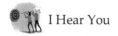 I Hear You

CUTTING THE CORD *(FORGIVING)*

There are times in life when we have to deny ourselves of things we desire for the betterment of those we love. If this happens, we must examine ourselves for feelings of resentment that are tied to the sacrifice. These feelings of resentment can be evidence that we blame others for the sacrifice and therefore have not forgiven them for that loss. Bringing those feelings to light is the first step towards cutting that cord and letting them go.

 I Hear You

Some individuals are reared in an environment in which they are rarely given the opportunity to express their feelings of hurt. After years of development under these conditions, that individual can become trained to store and hold tightly to feelings of hurt. We must make every effort to release those feelings once an issue is thoroughly discussed. Once clarification is reached, the offended party should be challenged to forgive the matter.

Repeated resurfacing of the incident may be attributed to lack of forgiveness by the offended party. It may also be a symptom of the fact that the parties are not having effective communication during which issues get resolved. One true indicator that the cord has truly been cut is whether or not the thought or visual presence of something or someone causes negative emotions to rush to the surface and negatively impact one's behavior or emotional status.

Past issues should not be brought forward into future discussions with intent to blame. It is not uncommon for someone to commit an insult to which he or she is also sensitive. When someone expresses feeling hurt by an action then at some point commits the same action, he or she is not necessarily issuing a double standard. When overtaken by hurt, people tend to respond in similar fashion. This makes it all the more imperative that we focus on what someone is feeling and address the feeling in real time. It is helpful to give consideration to what is currently happening and refrain from recalling a past action in order to downplay the current emotion or cast blame.

The best way to ruin a great today is to bring in a bad yesterday.

Doing so is likened to attaching a weight to a cord and dragging it through life. Stick to what is presently happening. Cut the cord. Repeatedly going into the past and bringing an unforgiven occurrence forward is a pitfall.

The person whose heart is hardened with unforgiveness may present us with one of the most difficult challenges in life—the sacrifice of the relationship. When spiritually bound to someone hurtful who understands what is negatively impacting the relationship, yet is unwilling to make changes, one will face difficult choices. Becoming a sponge and absorbing the hurt will ultimately lead to pain and suffering. As difficult as it may be, when one has exhausted all options and the relationship becomes extremely taxing, separating from that individual may be the best alternative. When not spiritually bound, severance may actually be the healthy option. People with hardened hearts who display a blatant disregard for loving, respectful behavior can become extremely hurtful and disruptive to daily life. When the negative tilt to the relationship is that severe, taking actions leading to self-preservation and self-protection may be the only choice.

Remember that forgiveness is a journey that begins with a commitment. We must be willing to take the first step toward forgiveness by making the commitment. Everything can change, so we ought to forgive often and love with all our heart. **Matthew 6:14** reminds us, "For if you forgive other people when they sin against you, your heavenly Father will also forgive you."

QUESTIONS

1. Do you challenge the person you have offended to forgive you for your error?

2. When offended, do you take the time to consider whether or not you have forgiven the person for the offense?

3. Do you make an attempt to come together and engage in communication that will enhance understanding when you find your relationship is strained with someone for reasons that you do or do not understand?

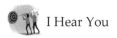 I Hear You

THE NEGATIVE TILT *(Failing to Take Responsibility)*

Failing to take responsibility for an improper action is a pitfall. It is one of the major contributors to the disruption of the emotional balance in all types of relationships. When an individual fails to take responsibility for an improper action—one that violates established rules or etiquette—he or she may also resist hearing or receiving information that supports the fact that the action is regarded as improper. This individual may make attempts to

argue that it was all right to take that action based on his or her emotional status at the time. There may also be a defense mounted that the manner in which the offense was called to the offender's attention was handled poorly. The violator may also use indignation as a defense.

One's emotional state does not relieve one of responsibility. Unless it is done harshly, the manner in which the offense is called to attention remains subjective. The efficacy of the statement in bringing the fault into focus is a more proper objective. However, all diligence must be taken to consider the receiver's sensitivities, if known, when bringing the issue to focus. Regardless of our intention, we are all responsible for the hurt that others experience as a result of our statements and actions.

Conflict will ensue and the emotional balance of the relationship will be disrupted when the responsible party fails to assume responsibility for the action. This action may cause other individuals with an understanding of the offense to reach out to the offender in an effort to bring clarity to the situation. As the offender continues to skirt the responsibility, he or she may feel like others are ganging up in opposition. The offender may begin to see the situation as becoming parental and harden his or her defiant position.

The more quickly we assume responsibility when we truly are the guilty party, the quicker we can resolve issues and thereby avoid hurtful statements, accusations, and behaviors. These negative actions can cause hurt, which tilts the relationship even more negatively. Failing to take responsibility is a pitfall. It is also a major contributor to stress and food for the cancer that consumes relationships.

KEY POINT

In a general sense, some things are considered improper in relationships; however, more specifically, there are practices that are improper to your relationship that may not be considered improper to another. Whenever an action is committed that violates established rules or etiquette, assume responsibility for that action as quickly as possible to prevent tilting the relationship in a negative direction.

 I Hear You

QUESTIONS

1. Do you quickly take responsibility when you discover that your speech or conduct has violated established rules?

2. Do you wait for the offended party to bring the offense to your attention?

3. What can potentially happen when one party fails to participate in the task of identifying negative cycles and fails to offer solutions?

 I Hear You

HONESTY *(Pure Honest Conduct)*

Being consistently honest and forthcoming when sending messages is also important. The receiver will begin to doubt the accuracy of the information received if there is a history of inconsistency. If someone notices emotions welling up inside of us by observing our nonverbal message and then inquires, replying "Nothing" when asked is dishonest. A more honest response is an acknowledgement that feelings exist followed by a statement that you are not ready to discuss the matter. Providing reassurance to the person making the inquiry will squelch the fire of concern and soothe any feelings of anxiety that may be emerging.

As the receiver, one must be diligent at clarifying received messages and avoid conditioning oneself to cast doubt routinely. This sort of skepticism has a negative effect on the communication cycle and makes it difficult for the receiver to hear. Routinely casting doubt on received communication without justification places one in a defensive position, which adds noise to the process and hinders communication. Doing so is yet another pitfall.

Most people will talk to someone about issues that are of concern. It is dysfunctional to bring the communication to an inappropriate source. Communication should first be brought to the original source for clarification. When repeatedly attacked, and attempts at clarification have failed, the sender of the original message may grow weary and choose to defend against the attacks or cease communication. The attacker may be oblivious to the effects of his attacks. He does not see himself as an attacker. Once offended by the perception, the attacker may see himself as the victim, causing him

 I Hear You

to attack in defense. This is usually a deeply-seated behavior that causes the attacker to react without clarifying.

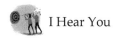 I Hear You

CASE STUDY (TELL ME THE TRUTH)

Bruce and Ellen have been married seven years. They have three adorable children, worship in a stable congregation, and are financially secure. Bruce is a prankster. He frequently approaches Ellen with fabricated stories to see if he can persuade her to buy in. She is very caring and will usually fall for any story with a strong emotional component. She is also a very vivid dreamer and will sometimes blend her dreams with reality. After seven years of marriage, Ellen is now unsure of whether she can trust the things Bruce tells her because of his frequent pranking. She is confused and frustrated. She has asked him to stop this behavior, but he continues because he finds it amusing. Feeling defeated, Ellen will sometimes succumb to nonverbal displays of emotion. When Bruce approaches her with genuine concern and asks, "What's the matter honey? You don't seem to be your normal self," her dishonest reply is usually "Nothing," which causes him to cast doubt regarding her truthfulness.

(See commentary in Appendix C)

 I Hear You

QUESTIONS

1. Is Bruce intentionally harming his relationship?

2. How is the lack of honesty affecting this relationship?

3. What actions can be taken to improve their situation?

 I Hear You

IMPERFECT PERFECTION (*TRYING TO BE PERFECT*)

One's quest for perfection is not the fault of one's significant other. It is not reasonable to think that we can perform in a relationship without making mistakes. This false notion can place an unfair burden on both parties in a relationship, since we are all imperfect. Striving for perfection causes one to magnify the inevitable setbacks that occur in life, both minor and major. Striving for perfection is another pitfall. This desire for perfection can lead to feelings of inadequacy. These feelings can sometimes be unfairly displaced onto our loved ones in the form of blame.

The need for perfection is not always taught. This need can stem from things that occur during our formative years. During this period of our development, if a child experiences negative reactions such as emotional or physical abuse from the authority figure, it can have a lasting, harmful impact. Children have a natural need to understand why. It is evident in the frequency with which they ask the question "Why?" Children look to trusted authority figures for understanding, which aids in their development. When a child suffers physical or emotional injury from a source they trust, the child tends to believe the incident occurred as a direct result of something he either did or did not do. This belief is usually followed by the rationale that if he performs better, the frequency of abuse will be lessened. With this thought in mind, the child begins to try and compensate through perfect performance in order to escape negative treatment. The harsh reality is, we are all imperfect. In later years, after this behavior is well-established, this subconscious need for perfection can be a source of conflict in interpersonal relationships. As this person begins

to try and please others, he or she may begin to blame others for what is viewed as a personal shortcoming. After all, he or she would not have fallen short if effort was not being spent trying to please someone else.

We should always try to display our true selves so we can be loved for who we are.

The inverse may also come to fruition as those in close personal relationships with this person begin to feel pressure. They may be viewed as having a lesser performance standard in various areas of the relationship. People to whom this person is an authority figure may begin to develop an altered self-esteem and self-image due to the repetitive feeling of inadequacy. They may in turn begin to blame this perfectionist for forcing them to be someone they are not.

It is easy for the person in search of perfection to remain constantly defensive and feel blamed or attacked when offered constructive criticism. This skewed impression will likely cast a right or wrong focus on most exchanges, which gives rise to conflict from the unwillingness to assume responsibility (if the focus is on right or wrong, someone must always be wrong). This orientation

 I Hear You

towards blame can result in stored anger and resentment, which add noise and dysfunction to the communication process. We are all imperfect and therefore require a measure of grace.

 I Hear You

CONTAINMENT BREACH *(Taming Hurtful Words)*

Name-calling is also a form of evil and is yet another pitfall. Whether we take ownership of this hurtful attack or not, calling a person names is a deliberate attempt to hurt that individual. It is an attempt to chip away at the armor that protects their self-esteem and self-worth. Name-calling sends the message that "You are not good enough. You are not measuring up to my expectations, so

I'm going to tear you down." This act falls into the realm of hurt people hurting people.

Emotional safety exists when we allow feelings to be what they are instead of what we think they should be.

When tempted to hurl hurtful words at another, we should take time to consider how we are feeling as well as the intent behind calling someone names. When we deliberately verbally attack another individual, we are often motivated by negative emotions such as anger, frustration, envy, and jealousy. The more swiftly we communicate that we are offended rather than engage in attacks via name-calling, the more likely it is that the issue will be resolved. It is an unreasonable expectation to think that someone can know what you are feeling without you properly stating it. Simply telling someone what he or she did is not the same as describing the action, then stating the feeling aroused by that action. One's display of anger does not state what one is feeling. Displays of anger are nothing less than threatening behaviors. Unresolved issues create discomfort and decrease the likelihood the two parties will demonstrate loving behaviors in each other's presence. When

 I Hear You

events occur that require the presence of both parties, the unresolved feelings are likely to disrupt the event.

After extended periods of exposure to hurtful words that attack our character during formative years as well as mature adult years, some individuals may develop an inaccurate view of themselves and their abilities. This can lead to mental as well as physical disorders. When tempted, we must make every effort to restrict the outflow of hurtful words before they breach containment and hurt another individual. When we feel the need to call someone by a name, we should be careful to only use the name given by his or her parents.

In **Matthew 12: 34-35** the Bible tells us "…For the mouth speaks what the heart is full of. A good man brings good things out of the good stored up in him, and an evil man brings evil things out of the evil stored up in him."

Sticks and stones can break your bones and name-calling will surely hurt you.

KEY POINT

It is important to consider how the words and actions we choose represent us. Negative speech

and behaviors will always represent us negatively. The inability to address the feelings of others will define us as insensitive. We simply must take the time to clarify messages before responding to them out of hurt. We must consider what we are feeling before we respond to another in a hurtful manner. If you suspect that your words/actions were processed inaccurately, it is within your best interest to contact the receiver of the words/actions and clarify the message received by that person. This will afford you the opportunity to replace it with the intended message.

CHALLENGE

Take a moment to evaluate whether or not you are in the practice of name-calling.

Have you identified what need this behavior meets for you?

 I Hear You

SHOCKING ELECTRONICS (*TEXTS AND EMAILS*)

Electronic communication such as text messages and email can be ambiguous and lack the compassion seen in face-to-face encounters. When possible, taking the time to communicate in person may convey the respect and compassion often needed to swiftly soften the receiver's emotional position. When conversation becomes crucial, coming together to resolve the issue conveys respect. When communicating electronically, both parties tend to become senders, which results in conflict. Some individuals lack self-control and will become more sarcastic, aggressive, and hurtful via emails and texts than they would have been when conversing face-to-face.

It is important to consider one's emotional state before sending an electronic message. Avoid texting or sending emails when frustrated or upset. Consider what information the message is intended to convey, and then assemble the words to say concisely that. It is also helpful to preview your message and examine it for assumptions, accusations, or preconceived notions. The receiver of messages with that type of content will likely become indignant and will offer clarification to what is seen as an erroneous message. Consider carefully the meaning of the words assembled in your message before sending them. It is important to show respect for decisions that individuals have made in governing their lives, especially if it differs from your position.

Do not text important responses; text messages are easily misinterpreted, which intensifies the problem. If someone gets emotional and sends you a long (one-sided) text, quickly delete it. Reading it may cause you to start developing misperceptions of your own, which may cause communication to spin out of control. Ask the person to call you if you think they are reasonable. Ask that he or she meet with you so you can properly communicate.

Encourage the person to divide the message into categorical thoughts and schedule a time during which both parties can address the thoughts contained in the message using healthy communication.

It is dysfunctional to fire an emotional shock waving discharge of emotions at someone and expect that person to give you proper feedback.

The receiver will likely be overloaded, which restricts hearing and comprehension. This renders the message ineffective. Scheduling a later time allows the individual space to contain the emotions, evaluate his or her thoughts, and communicate in a healthy fashion.

When involved with someone who has this unhealthy communication pattern, one must be cognizant regarding the steps taken to encourage that person to move away from it. Some individuals will refuse to change because they have never been allowed to have control and holding on to their dysfunctional position gives a sense of control. Some individuals may choose not to abandon their negative abusive patterns because they are comfortable and find it difficult to exert the effort needed to break the pattern of behavior. These individuals may be more willing to take from the relationship than give to it.

When an individual repeatedly refuses to adopt healthy communication, the relationship may ultimately reach a point where a decision may need to be made regarding keeping the connection or severing it. The toxic nature of this type of communication can be harmful to the emotional state of the receiver. If the relationship is one in which we are scripturally bound such as marriage, the answer to resolving communication issues will rest in one's patience and willingness to gently push for change.

During the life span of a marriage, there are periods of time during which we must be longsuffering and offer our partner grace.

QUESTIONS

1. Are you in the practice of sending emotional emails and text messages?

 I Hear You

2. What action should you take before you click 'Send' regarding texts and emails?
3. What steps can you take to avoid the conflict that arises from this practice?

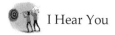 I Hear You

RIGHTFULLY WRONG (*The Need to be Right*)

As previously stated in the section "God's Gift to Man", feelings are neither wrong nor right, they just are. They are usually generated or stirred by something seen or heard. All feelings have a need. They need to be addressed. When someone trusts you enough to come to you and tell you how they feel, the responsibility on the part of the receiver is to listen for the feeling words and address the feeling that was expressed. When someone takes time to express how he or she feels, the unspoken message in this action of the sender is, "I trust you to be sensitive enough to respond lovingly to what I am feeling." Failure to do this will lead to mistrust and the sender will become more reluctant to share his or her feelings with this receiver due to the lack of sensitivity.

This insensitivity is a form of hurt and a definite pitfall.

The proper response becomes even more important if you are responsible for the action that generated the feeling. When given the opportunity to offer comfort and soothing to someone in emotional pain, one should address the situation with sensitivity. One should become an attentive listener and direct one's focus on identifying the emotion with the goal of deflating the emotional pain bubble. When blinded by the need to be right, one can lose focus of the emotion pain and begin to defend oneself. This action removes the focus from the emotional pain and places it on self. The sender, eagerly seeking comfort, will immediately see this shift and the pain will further intensify. As the receiver, one should realize that this action will create mistrust in the sender and cause one to be

 I Hear You

viewed as insensitive. Years of enduring this type of neglect can cause emotional scars that lead to compressed feelings and, eventually, anger.

Being responsible for arousing feelings does not always equal being wrong. However, failing to listen to the feelings of another and address them puts you in a position of error.

CASE STUDY *(You First)*

Paul and Angie have been married for over 25 years. They have three children. Their youngest daughter, Charlene, a sophomore in high school, is the only one remaining at home. She is very active in school and frequently needs to be picked up and dropped off. Angie will usually arrive early for pickup then wait for Charlene to come out. Paul is typically busy and prefers to arrive five minutes after pickup time so his downtime is minimal. One day after mutually agreeing that Paul would pick up Charlene, Angie approached Paul 15 minutes before scheduled pickup and asked, "Aren't you going to pick up Charlene?" The destination was eight minutes away. Paul looked up from his laptop. "I am going to pick her up," he replied firmly. Paul felt a little annoyed, because both he and Charlene had discussed with Angie that her

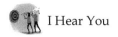

nurturing nature was causing her to seem like a helicopter mom, and requested that she reduce the hovering and allow them to have some space. Paul left his usual five minutes after scheduled pickup time in order to give Charlene time to put things away and say good night to friends. When he arrived, Charlene had been waiting for two minutes.

While on the way home, Paul processed his interaction with Angie. He realized his reply was a little firm and he could have chosen his words more carefully. She was already asleep when he arrived home with Charlene. He knew she would already be at work when he awakened the next morning. The next day, Paul made it a point to call Angie at work when he knew she was usually settled. He recalled the exchange, explained to her that he could have chosen his words more carefully, and expressed that he was sorry. "Thank you so much," she replied. "I was going to say something to you about that."

(See commentary in Appendix C)

QUESTIONS

1. Was Paul wrong for taking his initial position?

2. How did Paul demonstrate sensitivity in this interaction?

3. Why was it important that he take action as soon as possible?

Many individuals have compressed feelings that need to be addressed. Not all situations have a right or wrong basis, but someone or something is always responsible for actions that remove the scab covering the feelings, thus allowing them to flow out. The lack of sensitivity needed to address the feelings of another is a form of the cancer that consumes relationships. In order to become a skilled communicator, one must be willing to focus on the message before the desire to feel right.

Take note that if you have difficulty expressing your feelings to others when they are stirred without attacking, the focus will be removed from your feelings as the receiver is forced into defending against your attack. At the appropriate time, state what happened and the feelings that resulted from the precipitating event. This places all focus on the spoken feelings.

Nothing else needs to be said in order for the receiver to get the message. Try to limit the words spoken to what happened and the feelings

aroused by the action or words. After stating the feelings, simply pause and wait for the receiver to give feedback.

This will limit the opportunity for conversation to lose focus and shock wave out of control.

Individuals with an unhealthy concern for being right are often unwilling to assume responsibility. They seem to have a limited ability to hear the spoken message. This could be because they are focused on self, which yields difficulty with empathizing. This focus not only limits their ability to hear; it renders them insensitive. When individuals lack the compassion it takes to focus on spoken feelings, they will sacrifice interactions that can lead to greater intimacy. They will often confuse the performance of this compassionate act (giving focus to the spoken feelings) for an admission of guilt. This lack of compassion will often be processed as hurt by the opposing party when the feelings go unaddressed.

Simple responses to expressed feelings can be: "I wasn't aware that you were feeling that way. Now that I know, I'll look out for that next time." Or, "I am sorry my actions stirred those feelings in you. It wasn't my intention." Refusing to address stated

feelings due to concern for being right puts one in a position of error. This level of insensitivity can be attributed to a lack of awareness or it may also be connected to a hardened heart. Children who reach adulthood having never been taught this sensitive act can unknowingly be emotionally abusive to varying degrees.

The person who chooses to reflexively focus on right and wrong will likely choose to defend before addressing another's feelings when they are clearly stated. Remember, feelings are neither right nor wrong, they just are. The irony here is that the unhealthy desire to be right causes the person to take clearly wrong actions, which in turn intensifies the need to be right, resulting in a vicious cycle. The person possessing this burdensome desire will likely be prone to making accusations in order to shift the focus away from his or her deficit.

It is also worth noting that individuals who are prone to sudden outbursts of anger will unwittingly train the receiver to quickly explain his or her position or train the receiver to approach conversation in an indirect manner. The receiver engaged with this person may appear not to be listening, but is likely suffering from the anxiety brought on by the pattern of sudden, angry outbursts. The quick explanations offered are in fact part of a defensive coping mechanism used in an effort to avoid the hurtful, angry outbursts. The irony here is that a self-driven cycle is created. People who exhibit angry outbursts are seldom heard because of the anxiety generated by this negative form of communication. Sadly, this individual usually becomes angry when he or she feels unheard, which leads to more angry outbursts.

KEY POINT

We are all responsible for—and therefore to some degree, defined by—the actions we choose or refuse to take when addressing sensitive situations. Choosing to disregard the feelings of others when they are brought to us causes us to be seen as someone lacking compassion. We may also be viewed as insensitive. When we lack compassion, empathy, or sensitivity, we may frequently take actions that have the potential to erode our most intimate relationships as we insult and hurt our loved ones. These negative actions are part of the cancer that consumes relationships.

QUESTIONS

1. Do you feel the overpowering need to be right?

2. Does this need cause you to twist the facts of a situation so you can appear right?

3. Do you become angry when you discover that you are indeed wrong?

4. How can you eliminate this behavior?

 I Hear You

FOUNDATIONAL PRINCIPLE (*CORE CONCEPT*)

The sum of life's experiences can cause individuals to develop sensitivities, which in turn leads to the development of filters that impact hearing. These filters can disrupt hearing, causing men and women who hear the same set of words to process the meanings of those words differently.

Inference

During episodes of communication it is more important to place the focus on understanding the

message sent by the sender than one's interpretation of that message. This avoids the conflict that occurs when the message sent is replaced by the receiver's perception. It also ensures that the message is heard.

Effective communication requires the sender and the receiver to be fully aware of what he or she is feeling.

After developing a concise message, the sender must then approach the receiver with the intent to give information about his or her feelings, or to investigate the receiver's understanding of the message previously received. This effort is to ensure that he or she does not attack the receiver.

If you are the receiver, failure to clarify the message received (verbal or nonverbal) implies that one's misperception of the message is more important. This failure also nullifies the intended message and replaces it with one's perception of it. This action is a form of disrespect. Committing this action forces your misperceptions upon the sender as if they are factual. This action fails to consider the sender's message. The sender in this instance will try to clarify and may become indignant if not heard. The more the receiver pushes his or her disrespectful assumption without addressing the message received, the more the conflict will intensify. Always ask questions quickly to eliminate misperceptions and avoid accusing the sender of delivering the wrong message.

The more quickly the misunderstanding is clarified, the fewer subsequent misperceptions there will be to address. It is easy to embed yourself in a position that has not been clarified if you dwell on it without investigating first. This action is a huge obstacle to healthy communication. One must simply learn to ask questions before solidifying an opinion.

KEY POINT

Each time we approach someone with conversation, we should offer that person 100% of the respect to which they are entitled.

Properly stated, that is 100% respect applied to each instance of communication. To approach someone in a disrespectful manner with a conversation full of assumptions and misperceptions is not just hurtful, it is a flagrant injustice. Personal emotions from an earlier conversation should not be allowed to influence the current one.

 I Hear You

It is a selfish act to allow past emotions to have an effect on present conversation. It also implies that the previous issue was unresolved or not forgiven. Always take time to bring emotions in check before approaching another individual. Ask questions to be sure one's understanding of the intended message is accurate.

It is important to realize that communication will never be perfect and therefore we should not expect it to be. Much emphasis should be placed on the following:

- Gaining an understanding of the areas of difficulty regarding our individual communication style.

- Trying to gain an understanding of how our words and actions contribute to the difficulty during the process.

- Knowing how to go about taking responsibility for our contribution or the lack thereof.

While acknowledging that there is a level of difficulty involved in limiting our response to some emotions, the goal is to limit any response that is emotionally charged.

 I Hear You

REMEMBER THE MODEL

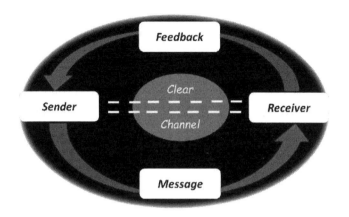

MODEL UTILIZATION

1. Parties are engaged in conversation and one takes offence to something heard. The offended party (receiver) replies, "This is what I just heard you say to me…. It caused me to feel…." The sender of the original message then listens and clarifies the message sent. It is advised that these conversations take place in private in order to avoid the influence of an uninvolved presence. Feelings tend to intensify when an insult occurs in the presence of others, so it is best to eliminate this factor when able. Override your filters and establish change.

2. You are engaged in some type of action and an act seems offensive to you. Ask, "What did you mean by that action…? It caused me to feel…." Do not make an accusation. Listen for the person's intent and acknowledge it (listen and believe). Avoid defaulting to anger without proper understanding. Once intent is understood, it is helpful to state how the message was taken and why. This helps the sender see what you are reacting to and enhances understanding.

3. When you are about to engage in a conversation you believe will be challenging, the sender starts the cycle by establishing the topic and sending the first message. It may be helpful to state, "I want to discuss this using the Communication Tool."

Approaching someone with strong language, tone, and demeanor when they do not realize that you are hurt or why you are hurt will deliver a firm insult, causing discomfort to the receiver of that message. This action makes the sender responsible for the sequence of events that follows. When the receiver fails to effectively listen, thus not clarifying or addressing the received message of feelings or hurt, the receiver is responsible for the sequence of negative events that follows.

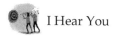

CONCLUDING WORDS (*IT'S IN YOUR HANDS*)

This model of communication is designed to change the way you hear/listen by removing your filters. Pay attention to how you think and formulate perceptions to messages you hear. Do you take time to clarify your understanding before responding? Have you brainwashed yourself with unfounded ideas that color the messages you hear? Resist the urge to go back to old styles of communication simply because the action is what you are used to.

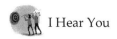 I Hear You

Each time you push your views/assumptions instead of asking clarifying questions and listening for the answer, the other party feels accused. Accusations hurt. Hurt builds defenses/filters. Filters impede healthy communication. Evaluate your message, tone, and actions for hurtful content and eliminate it. You have the power to eradicate the cancer from your relationships. The power to accomplish great things in your relationships is in your hand. Change your paradigm. Allow the healing to begin. You owe it to the next generation. Communication is seldom perfect; however, knowing how to navigate your way around the pitfalls will strengthen your relationships and protect those whom you love.

APPENDIX A

EXPRESSIONS OF FEELING

1. No
2. No
3. Yes
4. Yes
5. No
6. No
7. No
8. Yes
9. No
10. Yes
11. Yes

 I Hear You

ATTACK VS. OPINION

1. O
2. A
3. O
4. O
5. A
6. A
7. A
8. O
9. A
10. A

APPENDIX B

TEST 1

1. What type of interactions do we debrief? **Positive as well as negative.**
2. When a statement of feeling is properly made, it places ownership of the emotion on the **sender** or owner of the feeling.
3. When someone expresses a feeling, what are two things the receiver is expected to do?
   a. Give **feedback** pertaining to the **message.**
   b. Address the **feeling** heard.
4. What does expressing the feeling without making an accusation do for the receiver? **Allows the receiver to listen and focus on the message without feeling attacked.**

5. Why is shoveling to uncover the feelings of someone reluctant to share them contraindicated? What should we do instead?

   It allows them to remain complacent. Encourage them to state feelings using feeling words.

6. When communicating, why are we encouraged not to rage or display threatening behaviors?

   Threats take the focus away from the message.

7. The absence of communication or its delay is equal to or worse than ineffective communication because it allows issues to **fester** which leads to other **misperceptions.**

8. Other than conveying information, the primary goal of communication should be to avoid or **repair hurt.**

9. One's negative reaction to a present action or statement is usually tied to what?

   Something that happened in the past and was stored away as hurt.

 I Hear You

10. According to the foundational principle of our communication model, each individual is charged with the responsibility of confirming the meaning of the words spoken before **responding** to them.

TEST 2

1. Ineffective communication impacts relationships negatively by creating **misunderstandings.**
2. **Emotions** make a poor engine because they will usually run the train right off the track.
3. Hurt people tend not to think clearly and therefore require an additional measure of **grace.**
4. Each individual is charged with the responsibility of confirming the **meaning** of **words** heard before reacting to them.
5. When communicating with someone who is hurt, the receiver is focused on listening for the **feeling** that is stated.
6. When communicating it is important to remove all **noise** from the setting.

 I Hear You

7. The **attacker** is usually a poor listener who believes the contrary.

8. The **attacker** usually thinks he or she is a **victim** but truly is the aggressor.

9. The **sponge** will usually choose to absorb the unfair treatment of others despite feeling mistreated.

10. The **ostrich** openly admits to disliking confrontation and will purposefully try to avoid it.

11. The **diplomat** will seek conflict resolution quickly and effectively solves problems.

12. The message is the property of the **sender**.

APPENDIX C

CASE STUDY (THE DINNER INVITATION)

Susan quickly made assumptions, drew conclusions, and then verbally attacked Dwayne. She later allowed her feelings to override her judgment and engaged in spiteful behavior, which in turn hurt her husband. She would have been most effective if she asked questions that she could use to gather information and then expressed to him how she felt based on the sequence of events.

Dwayne failed to take responsibility for not passing on the invitation. He displayed no sensitivity when he noticed the change in her mood. He also failed to offer her an apology and ask her to forgive his actions.

CASE STUDY (THE TOILET PAPER INCIDENT)

Paula's reaction may seem like just a simple misunderstanding, but it is not. She is feeding a very complicated cycle of hurt. She took a very selfish position by failing to investigate her husband's position.

- She attacked him verbally with hurtful accusations.

I Hear You

- She never stated to him in a respectful manner what she was feeling and why.
- She accused him of: not caring what she liked, only thinking of himself, being inconsiderate, and already losing interest in her.
- She engaged in spiteful behavior: no kiss, cut off communication.

It is worth giving focus to the fact that if Paula continues down this path, her relationship will suffer. She demonstrates that she has already begun to brainwash herself in the false notion that her husband is losing interest in her. Years of this pattern of making assumptions against her husband without clarifying them can cause her heart to harden against him. She has already demonstrated an ability to cut off communication while she adheres to false ideas that cause her self-inflicted emotional pain. This continued pattern has the potential to make her relation susceptible to outside intrusion.

CASE STUDY (SELECTIVE SOOTHING)

Cindy's reaction to Carlos is less than effective. She did not demonstrate any concern for the way

Carlos was feeling after she called him a pig for leaving dishes in the sink. When approached by her son, who had injured his hand in the cabinet door, she very quickly addressed his pain by offering him comfort. She then displayed insensitivity by ignoring the hurt Carlos felt, which had resulted from the manner in which she spoke to him. It is clear that she has the ability to be sensitive but chooses to be selective with administering comfort.

Carlos approached her because he was in pain. He walked away with compounded emotional injury. This type of injury has the propensity to cause people to withdraw, thereby protecting self from further emotional trauma. This repeated pattern can have a profoundly negative effect on relationships.

CASE STUDY (WHERE IS THE LOVE?)

As a child, Cory was not prepared at home to be an effective communicator. He was not encouraged to express what he was feeling, so he did not develop the proper skills. When he became challenged to express what he was feeling, he did what he was accustomed to doing: he shut down. Due to the sudden attacks he faced at home and the oppression he experienced when it came to expressing his feelings, he felt safer when he kept his words to himself. His refusal to open up created a disconnect between him and Elizabeth.

Cory's hunger for emotional support drove him away from home prematurely. He was emotionally immature and financially unprepared. Both of these factors add stress to a relationship. When he found himself back in an intimate relationship, he did what he was trained to do. He turned inward, which caused many other issues. His wife was starving for emotional support, while he began to feel burdened.

 I Hear You

CASE STUDY (The Aftermath of Hurt)

The union of this couple was bound to be complex because of their backgrounds. Cheryl's parents were away from home often and she spent a lot of time without proper supervision. When they were there, they doted on her, but were also too protective, which curbed her maturing process and caused her to be self-focused. The lack of structured communication coupled with frequent unwarranted attacks yielded a defensive posture and anxiety with being confronted. She became rebellious and was naturally drawn to a bad boy who treated her badly. The pain of her experience led to her self-medicating. She truly did not know herself and was not ready for a serious relationship. This led to her negative reactions to criticism and people-pleasing behaviors. She saw criticism as a personal attack. Her lack of identity made it hard for her to stay on task, which in turn made her look flighty. Her attention span was short and her focus was short-sighted. This behavior brought negative criticism that angered her because she saw herself as failing. If she was unable to see herself, she was definitely unable to see what was going on with Danny. She looked to him for help, but she resented him because he seemed so focused and driven.

Her husband Danny was also self-focused due to the abuse he had suffered at the hands of his mother. He longed for maternal love and emotional support, which he sought from Cheryl. He subconsciously processed Cheryl's inability to stay on task as a lack of interest in him. This, in turn, meant she did not love him. His fulfilled prophesy reminded him of his mother, whom he tried desperately to please in order for her to demonstrate love for him and limit her abuse. It is easy to see how he ended up in an affair, for which he later blamed his wife. After all, she wouldn't listen to him, nor would she give him what he needed. He punished her with behaviors and spitefully neglected her. He became his mother. His need for love, which he wanted to be fulfilled through the performance, would never be satisfied. This drive made him a perfectionist; doing it right the first time meant he would not suffer abuse. This quest made him destined to fail. He was insecure. Having things done his way and on his timetable made him feel secure. It also made him very controlling. In addition, it obscured his vision of how he could be more effective at leading his family. He could not see the pain he caused Cheryl and the children through his negative behaviors. Burdened with pain and misperceptions, he too began to self-medicate.

The union of these two people with poor self-image and a lack of identity is ill-fated and destined for conflict. If their emotional maturity had not been stunted by emotional and physical abuse, their perspectives may have been clearer. They came together with the need for help that neither could supply. It was easier to look without and cast blame than to look within and identify the source of their turmoil.

CASE STUDY (HELP ME SEE CLEARLY)

This case study with Jarred and Tangie illustrates what can happen when our failure to trust is combined with the practice of brainwashing ourselves in false notions. When we close our minds to input or negatively twist information as we process it, we run the risk of harming others as well as ourselves. There are dishonest, misleading people on this earth. However, the experiences that we have with a few of them should not cause us to become so fearful that we lose the ability to hear and properly process information.

CASE STUDY (I WANT IT MY WAY)

This case study with Nathaniel and his aunt illustrates what can happen when we are overly selfish. Nathaniel's selfishness cost him his marriage as well as his relationship with his aunt. He was verbally abusive to those who disagreed with him and seemed to lack the ability to see how his actions impacted others. When hurt, people have a tendency to seek protection by fighting back or stepping away.

CASE STUDY (TELL ME THE TRUTH)

Relationships cannot and should not be dominated by seriousness. However, we must exercise great care to make sure that when people are requesting a straight answer, they are given one. Refusing to give serious answers when they are requested, even when there is no malicious intent, can sometimes erode trust. When inquiry is made regarding our present emotional state, we should remain honest and forthcoming, avoiding the excuses that lead us in other directions.

CASE STUDY (YOU FIRST)

This case study illustrates that sometimes it is better to forego the need to be right and place the focus on that which is more important, namely the concern for the feelings of others. Paul and Charlene had addressed the excessive hovering that Angie was exhibiting. They explained how it was causing them both to feel restricted. However, Angie was honoring her nurturing nature. She was headed for bed and was concerned that Charlene might have to wait too long if Paul did not leave 15 minutes before the pickup time. She did not even realize that she had fallen back into the same behavior. After considering the events, Paul realized that it would take some time for her to become more cognizant of the things that they discussed. He overlooked his frustration and placed his focus on the possibility that she may have been offended by his firm tone. He put her first and issued an apology. He placed her first.

 I Hear You

APPENDIX D

COURSE EVALUATION

Please visit my website, www.PeterEDooley.com, to complete the survey.

Read each statement below and assign a personal score of 1-5 using the following scale:

1-Strongly Disagree   2-Disagree   3-Neutral   4- Agree   5- Strongly agree

1. I am now able to clearly identify my position in the communication cycle during an episode of communication and give appropriate feedback.
   1 2 3 4 5

2. I now have a better understanding of how my ability to express what I am feeling impacts my relationships. **1 2 3 4 5**

3. This book has given me useful tools for navigating around the pitfalls of ineffective communication. **1 2 3 4 5**

4. My relationships have strengthened as a result of reading and applying the principles in this book. **1 2 3 4 5**

 I Hear You

5. I have a better understanding of how my upbringing has impacted the way I communicate. **1 2 3 4 5**

6. The manual was a useful resource during the course. **1 2 3 4 5**

7. The informal around-the-table format was helpful for delivering the information.
1 2 3 4 5

8. The presenter demonstrated mastery of the theory content. **1 2 3 4 5**

9. The presenter addressed my questions in a manner that met my needs. **1 2 3 4 5**

10. I would recommend this course to friends and family. **1 2 3 4 5**

**Kindly leave additional comments at,
www.PeterEDooley.com**

Made in the USA
Columbia, SC
26 May 2018